INSIGHT ⊙ GUIDES

BHUTAN

POCKET GUIDE

Walking Eye App

YOUR GUIDES ... AVAILABLE THROUGH THE WALKING EYE APP

... your new includes a free eBook to your chosen destination, for the same great price as before. Simply download the Walking Eye App from the App store ... access your free eBook.

HOW THE WALKING EYE APP WORKS

... destination corresponding eBook for free. Just see below the grey bar ... content and then scan the QR code at the bottom of the page.

Destinations: Download essential destination content featuring recommended sights and attractions, restaurants, hotels and an A–Z of practical information, all available for purchase.

Ships: Interested in ship reviews? Find independent reviews of river and ocean ships in this section, all available for purchase.

eBooks: You can download your free accompanying digital version of this guide here. You will also find a whole range of other eBooks, all available for purchase.

Free access to travel-related blog articles about different destinations, updated on a daily basis.

HOW THE EBOOKS WORK

The eBooks are provided in EPUB file format. Please note that you will need an eBook reader installed on your device to open the file. Many devices come with this as standard, but you may still need to install one manually from Google Play.

The eBook content is identical to the content in the printed guide.

HOW TO DOWNLOAD THE WALKING EYE APP

1. Download the Walking Eye App from the App Store or Google Play.
2. Open the app and select the scanning function from the main menu.
3. Scan the QR code on this page – you will then be asked a security question to verify ownership of the book.
4. Once this has been verified, you will see your eBook in the purchased ebook section, where you will be able to download it.

Other destination apps and eBooks are available for purchase separately or are free with the purchase of the Insight Guide book.

TOP 10 ATTRACTIONS

TAKTSANG, THE TIGER'S LAIR
The most sacred place in the kingdom, perched on a vertiginous ledge above the Paro valley. See page 31.

TSECHUS
Colourful Buddhist festivals held in monasteries with jesters and dancing monks. See page 37.

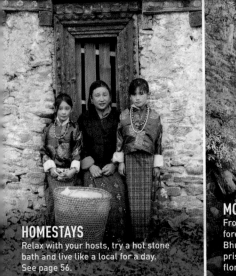

HOMESTAYS
Relax with your hosts, try a hot stone bath and live like a local for a day. See page 56.

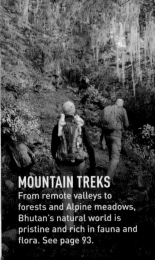

MOUNTAIN TREKS
From remote valleys to forests and Alpine meadows, Bhutan's natural world is pristine and rich in fauna and flora. See page 93.

PUNAKHA DZONG
In the ancient capital, this splendid fortified monastery is poised at the confluence of two rivers. See page 45.

ARTS AND CRAFTS
Watch young artists at work in the National Institutes in Thimphu or Trashiyangtse. See page 83.

BIRDWATCHING
Over 670 species of birds have been recorded, including the endangered black-necked cranes from Tibet. See page 49.

TRASHIYANGTSE
A beautiful remote valley in Eastern Bhutan with a tumbling stream and rice terraces framed by wooded slopes. See page 82.

ARCHERY
The national sport practised by men in traditional dress, accompanied by female cheerleaders and victory dances. See page 98.

FARMERS' MARKETS
Weekend markets in Thimphu and Paro are perfect for people-watching and discovering the local produce. See pages 29 and 39.

A PERFECT TOUR

Day 1–2

Paro

On your first full day in Bhutan, stroll around this charming town and explore the valley, the temples – called Lhakhang – and the old Drukgyel Dzong. Next morning, drive up to Chele La, Bhutan's highest road pass, then down to the secluded Haa Valley for a relaxing day.

Day 3

Thimphu

Drive to Thimphu, stopping briefly in Tacho-gang to walk across the restored medieval bridge, then discover the capital, see the dzong and other major sights, and have a break with coffee and cakes.

Day 6

Punakha–Bumthang

Back on the highway, head towards Central Bhutan, crossing the Black Mountains at the Pele La pass. Stretch your legs by the Chendebji Chorten, continue to Trongsa and marvel at the dzong perched on the edge of a ravine, before driving to Jakar, capital of the Bumthang district.

Day 4–5

Punakha

Drive to Punakha over the Dochu La pass and enjoy the panorama. Then head down to the semi-tropical Punakha valley to receive a blessing in the temple of the Divine Madman. On your second day, visit the dzong, picnic by the river and trek through paddies to the hilltop Namgyel Chorten. If you feel adventurous, go rafting on the river Mo Chu.

Day 7–8

Bumthang

Visit Jakar Dzong overlooking the Choekhor valley, Kurjey Lhakhang and the holy site of the Burning Lake. The next day, cycle or trek up the valley, visit temples and gompas – then have a relaxing evening. If there is a festival, allow time to attend.

OF **BHUTAN**

Day 14-17

Trashiyangtse–Bumthang

Overnight in Mongar then on to Jakar. From here, retrace your steps over the Pele La and turn off for the hidden Phobjikha valley. See Gangtey Gompa and the black-necked cranes in winter.

Day 11-13

Trashigang–Trashiyangtse

See Trashigang Dzong and explore the weavers' villages. Continue to the lost valley of Trashiyangtse, past the holy site of Gom Kora, and enjoy a homestay.

Day 9-10

Bumthang–Mongar–Trashigang

Long spectacular drive up to Trumshing La, the second highest road pass and gateway to the East. Overnight in Mongar and continue to Trashigang.

Day 18-19

Thimphu

Continue to Thimphu via Wangdue Phodrang. Next day, trek up to Cheri Gompa in the peaceful Begana valley, then indulge in last-minute shopping downtown. End with a bird's eye view of Thimphu from the giant Buddha Dordenma on the hilltop.

Day 20-21

Paro

Return to Paro in time for lunch and take in the dzong. On your final day, prepare yourself for the highlight of your trip and feel the spiritual vibes as you climb or ride a pony to the breathtaking monastery of the Tiger's Lair.

CONTENTS

INTRODUCTION

Nestling in the Eastern Himalaya between India and Tibet, Bhutan is a remote landlocked kingdom, stretching for 145km (90 miles) north to south and 300km (186 miles) east to west. Snow-capped peaks reach over 7,000 metres (22,965ft) in the west and north, petering down to rugged hills in the east, while in the subtropical south, jungle-clad hills lead down to the flood plain on the Indian border. Along the central strip are highlands laced in steep forested slopes and bucolic valleys dotted with market towns and isolated farms. Fast-flowing rivers carve their way north to south and the east-west highway, or lateral road, is a spectacular roller-coaster of high passes, deep valleys and dramatic gorges.

CULTURE

Druk Yul – 'the land of the Thunder Dragon' – lived in isolation until the 1970s, when the Fourth King cautiously opened the country's doors to its first tourists. Change was on its way, but the king vowed to protect the kingdom's cultural values to ensure 'Gross National Happiness' ahead of material gain.

With few exceptions, Buddhism remains the cornerstone of the Bhutanese identity and as guardians of religion, monks play a major role in society. Buddhist sanctuaries are omnipresent from glowing temples to roadside shrines, from the monasteries and religious fortresses known as dzongs to chortens, the oldest form of Buddhist monuments.

In this deeply religious kingdom, home to little more than 750,000 inhabitants, the royal family enjoys immense respect and affection, living a simple life close to the people. The royal couple and their son do not live in a palace but in a cottage with a garden, by the river near Thimphu's dzong.

CARING FOR THE LAND

True to Buddhist teachings, the Bhutanese regard the natural world as a gift to be cherished but not abused, and in this largely rural land, ongoing reforms aim to support farmers while respecting the environment. Dairy cattle wander unhampered in meadows fragrant with wild flowers and herbs, and the government has pledged its commitment to 100 percent organic farming within a decade or so. Crops vary according to altitude and soil: here lush luminous rice fields, there potatoes or maize, green vegetables, apples or tropical fruit – largely, though not exclusively, for domestic consumption. Nature yields wild berries, mushrooms and an amazing variety of medicinal plants, to pick as you need but no more. Energy needs are increasingly met by hydro-electric power, set up in cooperation with India,

Memorial chortens on the Dochula Pass

Harvested fields near Paro

and some 60 percent of the land is protected, including extensive forested areas.

There is no hunting or killing, even fishing is frowned upon, and in this safe environment, the wildlife is as diverse as the land, from tigers and elephants in the south to black bears deep in the forest or blue sheep and rare snow leopards in the high mountains. Where else but in a Bhutanese valley would overhead cables be banned to protect endangered birds? The flora follows suit, blue poppies – the national flower – and edelweiss, rhododendron, deciduous trees, blue pines and the lofty, emblematic cypress trees. From pastures and forest to the high mountains, spirits are believed to dwell in the natural world; Gangkhar Puensum, Bhutan's highest peak at 7,570 metres (24,835ft), is sacred, therefore no-one has ever climbed to the top.

PROGRESS AND TRADITION

The most significant change in modern times was initiated in 2005, when the Fourth Dragon King announced he intended to abdicate in favour of his son, but first, he wished to prepare the ground for a democratic government. There was much dismay as the people struggled to come to terms with the departure of their beloved monarch and a new political system many thought unnecessary. However, the new king (who gradually took office) visited every corner of the land to present and discuss the Draft Constitution. Elections were held in March 2008, resulting in a resounding victory for the pro-monarchy party, prior to the coronation which took place in November. But in 2013, following a number of mistakes by the fledgling government, the opposition came to power.

Now, the modern world is tightening its grip, traffic, cable TV, mobile phones, the internet revealing the wonders of the outside world and bringing new but often unfulfilled expectations. The pace is quickening but although Bhutan does not wish to be seen as a museum, traditional values are alive and well. In Thimphu, the capital, the building boom devours land in the valley, but on the hilltop there's a brand new temple with a giant golden Buddha to bless the people; cars choke up the streets at times, but on the roundabout a policeman directs the flow with the grace of a ballet dancer. Alongside new hotels, traditional architecture remains in

⊘ ROYAL ROLE

The *Kidu* tradition (wellbeing of the people) means anyone can approach the king and it is not unusual for His Majesty to stop at the roadside to chat to farmers, then follow up issues, or trek for days to meet villagers in remote areas. Respect implies distance, yet in a unique Bhutanese way, the royal family are genuinely involved with the people. After their wedding in Punakha, the Fifth King and his bride decided to walk most of the way back to Thimphu, 76km (47 miles), to greet the villagers lining the road to pay their respects. On a more dramatic note, when a major fire spread through the dzong in Wangdue Phodrang, the king promptly left the capital to join the locals struggling to salvage sacred items.'

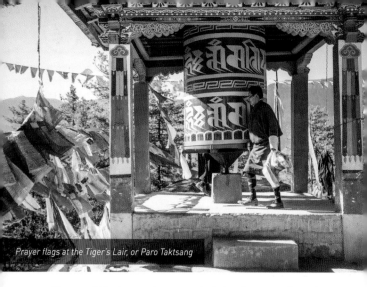

Prayer flags at the Tiger's Lair, or Paro Taktsang

evidence, all finely carved eaves and window frames and auspicious signs painted on the walls. Even in the new towns, where modern apartments are replacing the old fire-prone dwellings, there is a hint of traditional architecture. Meanwhile the cross-country highway is having a facelift, though traffic moves at the usual pace of 'no hurry, no worry'. The national dress is still worn with pride and Gross National Happiness has been enshrined in the Constitution. Some prefer to call it Gross National Harmony but for the gentle people of Bhutan, they go hand in hand.

TOURISM

Bhutan welcomes tourists as an all-season destination, though the climate varies with the altitude and the time of year. Summer brings the monsoon, particularly heavy in the south, while autumn tends to have clear skies and the best mountain views, ideal for trekking. Winters can be sunny but cold until spring returns, with masses of flowers splashing colour on the slopes. Only the highest peaks are covered in snow year round. But whatever the season, no visit to Bhutan is complete without attending one of the spectacular religious festivals held across the country throughout the year. Check dates when planning a visit.

Over the last decade or so, efforts have been made to increase tourism. New hotels have popped up alongside restaurants and coffee shops in Thimphu and beyond, the road linking Paro airport to the capital has been improved, cutting transfer time down to an hour or so, and Druk Air, the national carrier, now has to compete with the private Bhutan Airlines. Add a string of colourful celebrations such as the coronation, the royal wedding and the Fourth King's 60th birthday, and success has almost exceeded expectations. In a kingdom where the economy takes second place to cultural values, tourism is nevertheless a welcome source of revenue and employment. There are no current restrictions on numbers though regulations are in place to minimise the impact on the environment and local culture. 'High value, low impact' is the primary objective and for this reason, trips must be prebooked through registered operators; it is not possible to obtain a visa without doing so. Tourists are treated like 'guests' and in return, respect for local sensitivities is appreciated.

Value for money

Prices fixed by the government start at US$200 per night per person (US$250 in high season), including standard accommodation, meals, entrance fees, guides, private domestic transport and taxes. Supplements for small groups and luxury accommodation apply, while there are discounts for longer stays. All in, it offers excellent value compared to 'room only' deal in a western capital.

A BRIEF HISTORY

Steeped in Buddhist mythology, Bhutan's early history was recorded in religious texts but most were destroyed over the years by natural disasters and fires. There is little evidence of the first settlements, though it is believed that herders wandered through the land as early as 2,000 BC. The Bon animist tradition reached some of the valleys in the 6th century AD, while the rulers of Cooch Behar in India continued to exert their influence until the arrival of Tibetan Buddhism. No one knows exactly when Buddhism first appeared but the oldest temples are thought to be Kyichu in the Paro Valley and Jampey in Central Bhutan, built in the 7th century by the Tibetan king Songtsen Gampo. According to legend, he erected 108 temples in a single day to pin down a recumbent ogress.

⊘ DEITIES AND GODS

In Bhutan's colourful religion, worship goes beyond the three images of the Buddha: past, present and future. The Bhutanese prostrate in front of the Gurus, for without them no one would know the Buddha's teachings, and there are also saints, deities and enlightened beings, or bodhisattva, considered to be reborn to help others. Temples frequently feature the Three Gods, representing compassion, power and knowledge. Monks devote their life to religious practice accompanied by strict rules but for the ordinary people, this is a happy, easy-going religion. Life is a divine gift and enjoying every aspect of it, while respecting others, is showing appreciation. Temple deities in graphic embrace say it all.

Padmasambhava

BUDDHISM

In the 8th century the king of Bumthang in Central Bhutan sent for Guru Rinpoche, also known as Padmasambhava, to exorcise the demon that possessed him. The great teacher is said to have converted both the demon and the king to Buddhism then continued on his travels across Nepal and Tibet, before returning to Bhutan. According to popular belief, he was the 'second Buddha', incarnated as an eight year old child floating on a lotus blossom in India or in the Swat Valley – in today's Pakistan. The Guru's second visit marked a turning point in the history of Bhutan. Said to have flown on the back of a tigress, he landed on a precarious ledge high above the Paro valley, where after meditating in a cave, he defeated evil spirits and spread Buddhism across the land.

This may seem the stuff of legends but to every Bhutanese, it is real. Guru Rinpoche is the 'Precious Master' who enlightened the people and shaped their future. He left physical proofs of

The Thunder Dragon adorns the national flag

his visits, such as the 'terma' – hidden treasures preserving his teachings – and body imprints you can still see in parts of Bhutan. His eight manifestations are featured in many festivals.

MEDIEVAL TIMES

The 9th–10th century unleashed major turmoil in Tibet and following a wave of religious persecutions, a number of monks and aristocrats sought refuge in Bhutan. By the early 12th century, Tibet's religious revival had given rise to new Buddhist sects intent on spreading their teachings in the 'southern valleys', as Bhutan was called. Alongside the Nyingmapa, the Red Hat tradition founded by Guru Rinpoche, came several branches of the Kagyupa, among them the Drukpa, which is the main religious school in Bhutan today.

'Druk' refers to the nine 'thunder dragons' seen by a lama as he looked for an auspicious site to build the first Drukpa monastery. This was Ralung in Tibet. But forced to flee hostilities from rival groups, many Drukpa lamas came to Bhutan where they set up their own monastic orders. The Thunder Dragon eventually gave its name to the country and is featured on the national flag.

Throughout the Middle Ages, when Buddhism was the dominant force, religious leaders and chieftains clashed almost continuously as they fought to strengthen their influence, by sword or evil spell, but no commanding political figure emerged during that time. Yet two holy men rose to fame in Bhutan's religious history: Drukpa Kunley, the Divine Madman, monk and poet who 'enlightened' 5,000 women and is still worshipped to cure infertility, and the Nyingma saint, Pema Lingpa, ancestor of the royal family, who revealed the sacred dances he saw in his dreams, discovered many religious treasures and built monasteries in Central Bhutan. Also highly respected is Thangtong Gyalpo, the 15th century 'Iron Bridge Builder', who constructed 58 suspension bridges across Bhutan and his Tibetan homeland. Some are still used today.

UNIFICATION

In 1594, Ngawang Namgyel was born into a noble family in Tibet, where he became abbot of Ralung, the birthplace of the Drukpa. But at the age of 22, when his reincarnation was challenged by a provincial ruler, he escaped to Bhutan, said to be led by a deity disguised as a raven – the national bird on Bhutan's royal crown. There he took the title of Shabdrung and built a dzong at Simtokha in the Wang valley, the first of its kind to combine religious, civil and defensive roles. He repelled Tibetan invasions and fought against internal enemies, namely the 'Five Groups of Lamas' who belonged to rival schools. During his reign, dzongs and monasteries were built across

Dzongs

Poised on strategic sites, along rivers or on hilltops, Bhutan's iconic dzongs are formidable fortresses with small windows and inward-sloping walls. Inside is a maze of paved courtyards, ornate temples, monastic quarters and civic offices. They hold stunning religious festivals while Thimphu and Punakha also host royal events.

the land, a legal code based on Buddhist principles was introduced alongside a dual system of governance, with a state clergy led by the Je Khenpo, or Chief Abbot, and a secular administration headed by a 'desi'. The land was divided into three provinces, each one ruled by a governor or 'Penlop', and under the Shabdrung's leadership, the country was finally united. In 1651, he went into retreat in Punakha dzong and was never seen again. His charisma was such that when he passed away soon after going into retreat, his death was kept secret for 54 years in case the newly unified 'land of the Drukpa' fell apart.

WAR AND PEACE

It did not take long for such fears to be realised. Power struggles tore apart the new order, leading to centuries of internal strife and civil wars. Tibet invaded on several occasions before initiating a truce and eventually setting up diplomatic relations. In 1772 Bhutan invaded Cooch Behar to settle a succession dispute, but the British stepped in and forced the Bhutanese to retreat. Further battles followed until a peace treaty was signed in1774. The British returned the land they had conquered but the East India Company was given the right to exploit the forest in Bhutan. Skirmishes continued across the border, leading to an all-out war and British annexation of the Bengal Duars, the lowlands in Southern Bhutan, in 1864. At the Treaty of Sinchula the following year, the Bhutanese had to surrender large tracts of agricultural land.

In 1870 Jigme Namgyel, Penlop of Trongsa, emerged as a powerful leader but civil unrest continued until his son, Ugyen Wangchuck, defeated his rivals, firmly asserting his power while favouring closer links with the British. His role in settling a British-Tibetan dispute earned him the title of Knight Commander of the Indian Empire.

Ugyen Wangchuck was unanimously elected hereditary ruler by civic and religious leaders in 1907 and crowned 'Druk Gyalpo', the First Dragon King. Bringing long-awaited peace and stability to the kingdom, he pursued good relations with the British and at the Treaty of Punakha in 1910, secured his

'The War in Bhootan: The Burnt Palace of the Rajah of Saleeka', 1866

country's continued independence and increased monetary compensation for the Duars.

His son, King Jigme Wangchuck, reigned during the Depression and World War II but due to its isolation, Bhutan was not affected. The Second King maintained control over the country and improved the administration. In 1949, a treaty was signed with the newly independent India, who agreed not to interfere in Bhutan's internal affairs but reserved the right to be consulted in foreign matters. Some 82 sq km (31 sq miles) of the Duars annexed by the British were returned to Bhutan.

MODERN BHUTAN

Progress continued under the Third King, Jigme Dorji Wangchuck, who abolished serfdom, drew up a new legal code, set up a High Court, a National Assembly, an army and a police force, and restructured land ownership. Following the Chinese takeover of Tibet, he guided the country out of its isolation,

---

⊘ 'ONE NATION, ONE PEOPLE'

The population of Bhutan comprises a number of small ethnicities, many speaking their own language, and three main groups: the Sharchops, the original settlers in the east; the Ngalops of Tibetan descent in the west; and the Lhotshampas of Nepali origin in the south, brought into the country as unskilled labour. A policy introduced in the late 1980s required that all should embrace Bhutanese culture, such as wearing the national dress in public and accepting Dzongkha as the national language. This was strongly resented by the Lhotshampas, causing serious unrest and waves of refugees crossing the border into India.

finally joining the United Nations in 1971.

His son, King Jigme Singye Wangchuck, came to power in 1972 at the age of 16. Educated both at home and abroad like his father, he pledged to modernise the nation without compromising its values and faced a few problems along the way. After years of security threats on the Indian border, he headed an operation which flushed out Assam rebels in three days,

King Jigme Singye Wangchuck

but uniting the country's ethnic groups proved more difficult.

Yet during the 34 years of his reign, the Fourth Dragon King carefully steered his country into the 21st century. Druk Air, the national carrier, began operations in 1983 and the road network was vastly extended. Phone connections were improved and school enrollment approached a 90 percent all-time high. Free primary healthcare followed and life expectancy rose to 66 years, boosted by safe drinking water and smoking restrictions. New farming methods yielded better crops and alongside Gross National Happiness, Bhutan's GDP increased 15 fold in 21 years. Meanwhile, traditional arts and culture continued to flourish and national parks and wildlife sanctuaries were established to protect the environment.

Politics did not lag behind: the judiciary was modernised, greater power devolved to local authorities and contact with the outside world were encouraged on all sides. But above all, the Fourth King's most significant achievement was initiating the new constitution and setting up democracy through entirely peaceful means. The king has been granted the right of veto but in clearly defined circumstances, Parliament could pass a motion for abdication.

This was no easy act to follow for Jigme Khesar Namgyel Wangchuck, but the Fifth Dragon King was well prepared. In 2002 he had represented Bhutan at the UN General Assembly, addressing issues on children's welfare, he was invested Governor of Trongsa in 2004 and oversaw the final stages of democratisation prior to the 2008 elections. From the moment he came to power, he became the 'People's King', appealing to everyone, but especially to the young whose responsibility it would be, he said, to ensure the success of democracy. In his coronation speech in 2008, the king vowed not to rule but to 'protect as a parent, care as a brother and serve as a son'. He married his childhood friend, Jetsun Pema, in 2011 – sharing with her a passion for the arts, and the heir to the throne. His Royal Highness, The Gyalsey, was born in February 2016. Progress versus tradition is a fine balancing act but ever since the royal couple held hands in public, they have won the heart of every young person in the land.

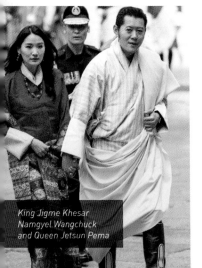

King Jigme Khesar Namgyel Wangchuck and Queen Jetsun Pema

HISTORICAL LANDMARKS

7th century A Tibetan king builds the first Buddhist temples in Bhutan.

8th century Guru Rinpoche visits Bhutan, spreads Nyingma Buddhism.

9th–10th century Religious persecutions in Tibet; lamas flee to Bhutan.

11th–14th century Buddhist revival spreads to Bhutan; Drukpa becomes the dominant school and sets up monasteries.

15th–16th century The Iron Bridge Builder comes to Bhutan; the Nyingma saint Pema Lingpa discovers sacred treasures; the Divine Madman spreads new ideas.

1616–1651 Shabdrung Ngawang Namgyel flees Tibet and unifies Bhutan, bringing law and order and repelling Tibetan invasions.

18th–mid-19th century Internal power struggles; confrontation with British.

1864–1865 Duar Wars with the British, settled by the Treaty of Sinchula.

1870s Jigme Namgyel emerges as the most influential leader.

1897 A major earthquake causes extensive damage across the country.

1907 Ugyen Wangchuck becomes the First King of Bhutan.

1926 Jigme Wangchuck becomes Second King of Bhutan.

1949 First Treaty of Friendship with India.

1953 The Third King, Jigme Dorji Wangchuck, sets up National Assembly.

1971 Bhutan joins the United Nations

1972 The Fourth King, Jigme Singye Wangchuck, comes to power.

1974 The first tourists arrive.

1985 Bhutan joins the South Asian Association for Regional Cooperation.

1988 The 'One Nation, One People' policy is launched, causing major unrest among southern people of Nepali origin.

1998 The king gives up some of his powers to an elected Council.

2006 The king confirms abdication, with aim of the crown prince introducing democracy.

2007 New Treaty of Friendship signed with India, Bhutan's closest ally.

2008 National Assembly elections won by the Bhutan Peace and Prosperity Party. The Fifth King, Jigme Khesar Namgyel Wangchuck, is crowned.

2013 The People's Democratic Party wins the elections.

2016 His Royal Highness The Gyalsey, heir to the throne, is born.

Horses at Paro Taktsang

WHERE TO GO

Bhutan can be divided into three sections, west, centre and east. Most visitors fly into Paro in Western Bhutan and those on a short trip will venture as far as Punakha. Two weeks or so will allow time to explore the central valleys and appreciate the spectacular scenery along the way. The eastern reaches may seem close on the map but bearing in mind the mountain road, the high passes and stunning panorama, the journey requires a leisurely pace to take it all in. The southern lowlands claim a few cities but tourism is still in its infancy here. Of special interest are the wildlife sanctuaries along the Indian border, but be prepared for basic facilities.

A note on opening times: Bhutan is a fluid kind of place, and where opening days or times are not specified in the text, you can assume that the sights will welcome visitors at any time, unless there's a ritual going on or the caretaker's gone out for lunch. Away from major tourist spots, the best thing you can do is to let your guide know what you want to see, and they'll make the arrangements. Sit back and relax...

WESTERN BHUTAN

Home to the only international airport in the country, Western Bhutan is the most visited region in the country and a true microcosm of all the kingdom has to offer. From the religious sites of Paro to remote valleys and from the gentle buzz of modern Thimphu to the historic capital of Punakha and the dramatic Black Mountains, the colour and beauty of this land will leave visitors longing for more. The scenery unfolds in slow motion, forever changing as the road wanders through

Etiquette

Visiting a dzong or temple requires appropriate dress, no short skirts or shorts, no vest tops or T-shirts (unless covered), no flip-flops, sandals or headgear. Short-sleeved shirts must have a collar. Remove your shoes before entering a temple and note that photos are not permitted inside.

semi-tropical valleys or climbs to mountain passes with unrivalled views.

PARO VALLEY

After the dazzling mountain flight from Kathmandu, landing in **Paro ❶** at 2,250 metres (7,382ft) greets you like a dream, with thickly wooded slopes, rice fields on the valley floor and the distinctive **Rinpung Dzong Ⓐ** (daily 9am–5pm) rising on the bank of a tumbling river. Built by the Shabdrung in the 17th century, then restored after a fire which destroyed many treasures, the 'Fortress on a Heap of Jewels' is accessed by a traditional wooden bridge, roofed with shingles and garlanded in Buddhist prayer flags. Like every dzong in Bhutan, it is a living place, home to a large monastic community who serve the people through prayers and rituals. The central tower is one of the finest in the kingdom while courtyards, galleries and temples reveal colourful mandalas and paintings such as the Old Man of Long Life or the Four Friends, elephant. monkey, rabbit and bird climbing on each other to reach fruit on a tree.

On the hill above Rinpung Dzong is **Ta Dzong Ⓑ** (Sun–Fri 9am–4pm), the circular watchtower housing the National Museum where crafts and ritual objects are displayed alongside jewellery, clothing, thangkas depicting gurus and saints and natural history items. There is a road to the top, but going on foot reveals excellent views of the valley, as well as **Ugyen Pelri Palace**, built in the early 1900s to resemble the heavenly residence of Guru Rinpoche. The palace is not open to the public, but the nearby row of white chortens is worth a picture. Be sure to walk around in a clockwise direction as according to holy texts, this ensures good karma.

Back in town, it is easy to wander around as Paro feels like a big village, where traditional buildings rise like works of art, willows whisper along the river and in the clear mountain air, prayer wheels tinkle in temples and shrines. Built by a Tibetan abbot, ancestor of the Shabdrung, the town temple, **Druk Choeding**  houses protective deities and the Buddha of the Future, while **Dumtse Lhakhang** was erected by the Iron Bridge Builder has three floors to represent hell, earth and heaven. As elsewhere in Bhutan, temples are not always open but if you look around, you might find a caretaker with a key.

Meanwhile, in the high street, a new crop of hand-icraft stores awaits visitors but those who venture into the lanes will find old-fashioned shops where chillies hang from the eaves and incense burners release their fragrance in the air. But for a genuine taste of Bhutanese life, nothing beats the Sunday market where farmers greet would-be custom-ers with beaming smiles, stained red by years of betel nut chewing, and entice them with tempting

Monks at Rinpung Dzong

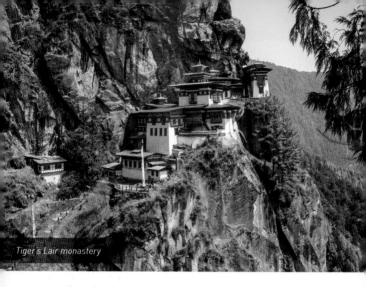

Tiger's Lair monastery

– at times intriguing – seasonal produce from curly ferns to aphrodisiac mushrooms.

Upriver, a short distance out of Paro, **Kyichu Lhakhang** Ⓔ has been rebuilt and extended over time, most recently with a temple sponsored by the Royal Grandmother. It contains a 5 metre (16ft) -high statue of Guru Rinpoche and iron links forged by Thangtong Gyalpo. In the main sanctuary are statues of the Tibetan king who built the original temple in 659 AD and – most precious of all – of Jowo Sakyamuni, the young Buddha, similar to the famous statue in Lhasa. Fourteen kilometres (8.6 miles) from Paro, the road ends at **Drukgyel Dzong** Ⓕ, little more than a ruin perched on a rock now, but in the17th century it was strong enough to keep the Tibetans at bay. Restoration is underway, scheduled to take until 2020, and in the meantime only the dusty courtyard is open. Nearby is a small settlement of wooden houses where, on the edge of the terraced fields, women wash their clothes at the pump and roast barley on an open fire. In this tranquil valley sprinkled with isolated farms, time seems to stand still, a world away from the town and its airport.

Yet just off the road is **Taktsang** ⑥, the Tiger's Lair monastery (daily 8am–1pm, 2–5pm) and Bhutan's best known icon. Named after Guru Rinpoche and his flying tigress, it defies imagination, even from a distance, clinging to the cliff face 800 metres (2,624ft) above the valley floor. It's awesome, mesmerising, but visitors who don't feel up to the climb can hire a pony to the panoramic half-way point. Should you decide to walk, allow at least half a day to make the most of the experience, climbing amidst blue pines and rhododendrons, stopping for refreshments or a hot meal at the viewpoint, then following the trail above the tree line in the footsteps of holy men. The final stretch involves a long flight of steps down to a waterfall that plunges into the chasm then up to the entrance gate on the other side. Leave cameras and bags in the lockers provided and be aware that you will need to remove your shoes several times. There is not much room on the ledge, but vertigo-sufferers can soon escape into a maze of temples swirling with gilded statues and multicoloured paintings. Pilgrims or tourists, no one can ignore the vibes, especially when the deep chanting of monks echoes around the walls.

West of town near the **airport**, a road climbs though a forest of spruce and larch to **Cheli La** ❷, at 3,810 metres (12,500ft), the highest road pass in the country. Up there above the trees, tall prayer flags flutter in the breeze and in clear weather the view extends to **Jomolhari**, the second highest mountain, and other snow-capped peaks close to the Tibetan border. On one side is the Paro Valley, on the other the **Haa Valley** ❸, beautiful and remote and the second-least populated district in Bhutan.

A large area is protected by the **Jigme Khesar Strict Nature Reserve ❹**, a mix of broad-leaved forest and lush meadows dotted with small lakes where the white poppy, found nowhere else in the world, grows to a height of 1.5 metres (4.9ft). No one lives in the reserve, which is connected by a biological corridor to the Jigme Dorji National Park to the north.

East of the reserve is a scattering of villages and the little town of **Haa** with its dainty houses, glowing temple and Indian army camp. A mountain stream rushes over white pebbles and guarded by the Hill of the Three Gods, the valley is bathed in legends and mystical rituals designed to appease the local deities. Wheat and barley are grown on terraced slopes, and rice in the lower reaches. If time allows, spend at least a couple of days here to gain an insight into local life and look out

View over Haa

for sacred rocks, hidden temples and caves where monks meditate in solitude. A two-day Alpine festival is held in summer to celebrate the local culture with traditional food and drink, masked dances, folk song and archery contests.

Then continue down the valley past the isolated Dobji dzong and join the Paro–Thimphu road at **Chuzom ⑤**. This is a major junction and a sacred site at the confluence of the Paro and Wang Chu rivers, protected by three chortens in different styles.

Masked dancer at the Haa festival

The main road south winds its way through the district of **Chhukha**, a scenic drive lined with waterfalls, heading from the cool mountains down to the sweltering lowlands and the border town of **Phuentsholing**, 141km (87 miles) from Chuzom. Heat, pollution, traffic: there is little to commend the town except to determined overlanders.

THIMPHU

It is 55km (34 miles) from Paro to Thimphu via Chuzom but before reaching the junction, most visitors stop briefly at **Tachogang**, where the more adventurous walk across the rickety iron chain bridge to the small temple on the hillock. Rebuilt as it was in the 15th century, the old footbridge is fun to tackle, though there is also a modern version for more sedate travellers.

At an altitude of 2,350 metres (7,710ft), **Thimphu** ⑥ is among the world's highest capitals, modern, lively but still full of traditional charm. Sprawling across a valley too small to accommodate an airport, it has started to creep up the slopes, having grown from village to city in less than 30 years. The current population is estimated at 100,000, boosted by a steady flow of young rural migrants lured by bright lights and dreams of government jobs. The **Clock Tower Square** has seating for concerts and other popular events, there are trendy bars and clubs downtown, enticing shops and stores along **Norzin Lam high street** and ATM machines so no one runs out of cash. Yet it is low-key by western standards, and new buildings can be no higher than six floors, attic included, ensuring a low-rise cityscape. South of town, the finely decorated petrol station

Tachogang's old footbridge

has retained its wow factor, unruffled by the new expressway easing traffic into the city. Traffic lights were installed but deemed unnecessary and intrusive, they were removed by public request. Wherever you are, you know this is Bhutan.

The city centre is a pleasure to explore on foot, but be aware of the altitude and take it easy at least for the first couple of days. Note also that most of the sights are located in the Greater Thimphu area. Transport will be provided by the operator, by far the best option on a short visit.

To the north, beyond the end of the high street, **Tashichho Dzong** (Mon–Fri summer 5.30–6.30pm, winter 4.30–5.30pm, Sat–Sun 9am–5pm) rises among flowers and lawns above the river Wang Chu. This is the summer residence of the main monastic community – known as the central monk body –

led by the Chief Abbot. Built by the Shabdrung when the original fortress became too small and enlarged in the 18th century to accommodate both monks and civil officials, it was damaged and rebuilt and once again renovated and extended in 1962, after the capital was moved to Thimphu by King Jigme Dorji Wangchuck. The project took five years to complete, without nails or written plans according to tradition, for the most holy sites are believed to be created in visions. The entrance depicts the Guardians of the Four Directions, the Divine Madman sporting a bow and arrow, the

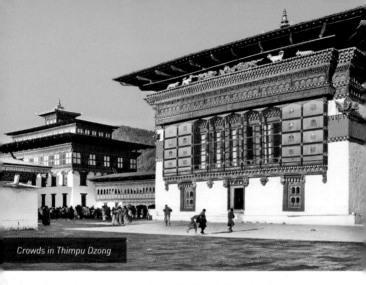

Crowds in Thimpu Dzong

legendary Four Friends, and other deities. Walking up the Great Staircase, notice the national crest and carved pillars before stepping out into the courtyard lined with civilian offices and festooned in lavish decorations. On the north side of the tower are the monastic quarters and courtyard where Lhakhang Sarpa displays mythical animals, mandalas and an impressive image of Guru Rinpoche. The large building fronted by a decorated porch houses the monks' assembly hall and its huge historical Buddha, while on the upper floor, a finely decorated chamber contains the king's throne. This was the seat of the National Assembly, which has now moved across the river.

On the 10th day of the ninth month in the lunar calendar, Thimphu Dzong is in festive mood, bustling with colour and life as locals come from far and wide to attend the 3-day-long *tsechu* held in honour of Guru Rinpoche. This is an annual chance to be blessed and earn merits, wear your finest clothes and meet family and friends you may not have seen for a long time. There are picnics by the river and back in the dzong, medieval-style jesters, or 'Atsaras', to liven up the lengthy proceedings with naughty tricks and explicit jokes, reminding the crowds about safe sex, study, health care and more. But it is first and foremost a religious occasion when laymen and monks in heavy brocade pounce and swirl on the flagstones in a flurry of bells, fierce masks and garlands of skulls. Long horns, cymbals and gongs chase away evil as tales of Bhutanese lore are brought back to life. *Tsechus* are held in dzongs and other monasteries and are sometimes preceded or followed by a Dromchen, a short festival usually dedicated to protective deities.

South of the dzong on Pedzoe Lam, the **National Library** (Mon–Fri 9am–1pm, 2–4pm, summer until 5pm) is home to an ancient collection of Dzongkha and Tibetan texts written on strips of handmade paper, held between wooden blocks and wrapped in silk. Print-ing blocks for books and prayer flags are on show alongside various items on Bhutan, the most excit-ing of which is the world's biggest book. The richly illustrated 'Bhutan' is over 2 metres (6ft) high and weighs 68kg (150lb). It cannot be borrowed but small copies are on sale for US$100. In the same

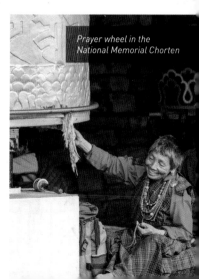

Prayer wheel in the National Memorial Chorten

area are the **National Institute of Traditional Medicine** (Mon–Fri 9am–1pm, 2–4pm, summer until 5pm), the **Textile Museum** (Mon–Sat 9am–4pm) and the **Folk Museum** (Mon–Fri 9am–4pm, summer until 5pm, Sat 10am–4pm) which displays traditional agricultural and household items.

In the town centre, the **Post Office** (Mon–Fri 9am–1pm, 2–4pm, summer until 5pm, Sat 9am–1pm) has a popular philatelic bureau, the best place to buy collectors' stamps – including personalised and talking versions. Meanwhile, down by the river north of the Coronation Park and stadium, the largest

☉ NATIONAL DRESS

Jeans might appear now and then around town but at festival time, the national dress is the ultimate expression of Bhutanese culture – far from a one-size-fits-all uniform, for there is plenty of scope for new designers to experiment with colours, patterns and silk or cotton materials.

Women wear an ankle-length *kira*, a single rectangular piece of colourful fabric wrapped around the body, fastened by a tight belt and a shoulder clasp, worn over a blouse with long turn-up sleeves and a short jacket, enhanced by jewellery, traditionally silver, coral and turquoise. Men wear a knee-length *gho* with a belt doubling up as a pouch and wide removable white cuffs on special occasions. Long socks are part of daily attire, but knee-high embroidered boots made of silk or cloth can be seen at festival time.

Tourists are not expected to wear the national dress but anyone who chooses to do so will find all they need on Norzin Lam, priced according to quality. If you need help to get dressed, hotel staff will be delighted to oblige.

Chillies for sale at the Thimpu weekend market

weekend market in the country draws farmers from all over the district and beyond. Allow plenty of time to browse the pristine hall where shiny red chillies mingle with purple banana flowers, freshly shelled peas, edible ferns, mushrooms, garlic, red rice, apples and tropical fruit according to season. Across the pretty cantilever bridge, the tourist market offers anything from temple horns and prayer wheels to wind chimes, textiles and strings of coral and turquoise beads. Many of these items are imported.

For something more authentic, visit the **Jungshi Paper Factory** (Mon–Sat 9am–1pm, 1.30–4.30pm, summer until 5pm) on the east side of the river or the **National Institute for Zorig Chusum** (Mon–Fri 10am–noon, 2–3.45pm, Sat 10am–noon, closed July, late Dec–Feb). Also known as the 'painting school', the Institute teaches the most promising students some of the traditional arts, once encouraged by the saint Pema Lingpa, who was himself a fine craftsman and artist.

Bhutanese crafts

Formally defined by the Shabdrung in the 17th century, the 13 Bhutanese arts and crafts include weaving, embroidery, stone-work, painting, bamboo work, carpentry, carving, wood-turning, clay work, bronze-casting, blacksmithing, paper making and crafting ornaments, mostly from silver, gold, turquoise and coral.

South of the town centre on Chorten Lam is the **National Memorial Chorten**, a striking white monument topped by a gilded pinnacle, built in 1974 in memory of the Third King, Jigme Dorji Wangchuck. It is one of the most popular venues for daily worship, containing religious paintings and statues, prayer wheels and a shrine dedicated to the late king. Chorten means 'Seat of Faith' and there are plenty of offerings to prove it: butter lamps, incense or ceremonial scarves. Equally important is **Changangkha Lhakhang**, perched on a ridge above town, where families traditionally bring their children to be blessed.

Northwest of Changangkha, bordering the stylish residential district of Motithang – the 'meadow of pearls' – the **Takin Wildlife Preserve** (Tue–Sun, 9am–4pm, summer until 5pm) is well worth a detour to see these unusual animals wandering in semi-liberty. According to legend, the original creature, seemingly with a goat's head and a cow's body, was created by the Divine Madman to demonstrate his miraculous powers. It is the national animal of Bhutan and although takins live in the wild, this is the best chance to see them close as they graze undisturbed under the pine trees.

Then, if you want a day out of Thimphu, drive north through the serene **Begana Valley** to the end of the road. There the right-hand trail climbs up to **Tango Gompa**, under renovation until 2018 and a good hour 's climb, unless one is brave enough to tackle the shortcut; and to the left is the path to **Cheri Gompa**. Either way, it is a good idea to carry sufficient water and a picnic, for there are no refreshments at the top. For Cheri Gompa, cross the tumbling river over the old covered bridge draped in prayer flags and allow up to an hour for a steep but delightful walk. In this inspiring site, monks meditate in solitude and nothing disturbs the peace but birdsong and butterflies. Cheri was built by the Shabdrung to house his father's ashes and no one could deny this is a resting place with a wonderful view.

Alternatively, on a ridge south of Thimphu – a 5km drive (3.1 mile) – **Simtokha Dzong** is another interesting sight boasting over 300 slate carvings, prayer wheels, a cosmic mandala painted on the ceiling, images of protective deities, and some

The National Memorial Chorten

The Buddha Dordenma

of the oldest murals in the country. Now home to the Dzongkha Language Institute, it was the first dzong built in Bhutan.

Across the valley, a road leads up to a hilltop where above the protected forests of the Kuensel Phodrang Nature Park, the **Buddha Dordenma**, seated 'on a throne with a thunderbolt', reaches 51.5 metres (168.9ft), making it one of the highest such statues in the world. It is made of bronze covered in gilt and inside the Buddha's seat, the vast prayer hall contains 125,000 small statues. The main statue was completed in September 2015, in time for the Fourth King's 60th birthday, and it is said to fulfil an ancient prophecy to bring peace and happiness to the world.

PUNAKHA

The 76km (47 mile) drive to Punakha takes a good three hours, allowing for breaks along the way. Climbing through apple orchards, the first stop is likely to be to buy fruit at the roadside; then there are views of monasteries high above the valley, just begging for photos, and at 2,890 metres (9,481ft), a checkpoint in the village of Hongtsho. The road continues through oak trees and feathery blue pines until you reach the **Dochu La pass ❼**, with magnificent views at 3,140 metres (10,301ft), weather permitting. But even when the mountains are shrouded in mist,

Dochu La is steeped in magic with its tall prayer flags climbing up the slopes, the 108 chortens to circumambulate – walk all the way around – seven times in a clockwise direction (no mean feat at this altitude), and a relatively new temple on the hillock, partly built by volunteers to earn merits. In Bhutan, work is often regarded as a way to express gratitude for the gifts of nature, and when a sacred venue is involved, blessings for the present and the afterlife are reward enough.

There is also a large cafeteria on the pass where visitors can relax with a drink and a snack or buy a few (fairly expensive) gifts before heading down through a forest of cypress, firs and the daphne bushes used for handmade paper. At Lamperi, 11km (6.8 miles) below the pass, is the entrance to the botanical garden, set within the **Royal Botanical Park**, inaugurated

⊙ CHORTENS

A chorten, or stupa, is said to represent the Buddha's mind and is therefore sacred. The first chortens were built to receive the Buddha's relics which were split after his death. Today chortens are erected to honour important figures, earn merits for the dead or subdue demons. The different parts of the monument represent the five elements, earth, water, fire, air and ether. Some contain chapels but most are closed structures and devotions consist in circumambulating several times in a clockwise direction. Building a chorten brings blessings, but this must be done according to tradition as sacred items and a 'tree of life' are placed inside. Large whitewashed chortens mirror the Nepalese style, small stone chortens are Tibetan and square chortens with a red stripe below the roof are traditionally Bhutanese.

Dochu La

in 2008 and the first of its kind in Bhutan. The Park displays all 46 species of wild rhododendrons that grow in Bhutan and a three day festival is held in April or May when the flowers are at their best. Then below 2,000 metres (6,561ft), the vegetation becomes almost tropical, a mix of bamboo, chir pines, banana plants and orange trees. Chortens and mantras painted on the rocks ensure a safe journey and at Metshina junction, you leave the highway and head north to continue the descent into the green **Punakha valley** ❽. At around 1,300 metres (4,265ft), the former capital is the winter residence of the central monk body and the venue most closely associated with Drukpa Kunley, the Divine Madman.

Before you reach town, **Chimi Lhakhang** beckons on a hillock among the rice fields where the most popular saint in Bhutan built the original monument. Access from the road is on foot across the paddies, muddy at times, and through a couple of hamlets where pastel-coloured phalluses painted on exterior walls leave no doubt as to the madman's passion. All he tried to do, they say, was to liberate the people from strict conventions which limited life's enjoyment and to this day, such symbols are considered auspicious, ensuring healthy children and good harvests. It is a 20–30 minute walk to the temple, where a monk blesses locals and visitors with a wooden phallus, a peacock feather and a few drops of holy water. Entrance is free but as in most temples, a small donation is welcome.

Punakha Dzong (winter daily 9am–noon, 2–5pm, summer daily 9am–1pm, 2–5pm), known as the 'Fortress of Great Happiness', is for many visitors the most photogenic dzong in Bhutan. Poised like a ship at the confluence of the Mo Chu and Po Chu rivers, it dates back to 1637, following a prediction by Guru Rinpoche that a fortress would be built below an elephant-shaped hill. On one side, it can be reached by a covered bridge over the Mo Chu and on the other side, by a long dizzying suspension bridge swinging above the Po Chu. The dzong includes 21 temples, courtyards and halls and a six-floor-high central tower. Most important is Machey Lhakhang, which contains the remains of the Shabdrung and the '100 pillar congregation hall' decorated with paintings and statues. Over time, the dzong has been damaged by floods, earthquake and six fires, but it repelled a Tibetan army intent on recovering a precious relic

The Punakha thongdrel

A thongdrel is a giant appliqué thangka representing religious figures. This one is the largest, 6,000 metres (19,685ft) of silk brocade and the work of 51 artists. At festival time it is unrolled from the dzong rooftop, blessing all who set eyes on the sacred image of the Shabdrung.

brought to Punakha by the Shabdrung. The event is re-enacted every year during the Dromchen festival in late winter, culminating in the unfurling of the thongdrel (see box).

Some 5km (3 miles) south of the dzong is Khuruthang, the new town where facilities line the right-angle streets, but the old Punakha valley is more attractive, a lush hideaway where one can explore the countryside from forested slopes and sleepy villages to pastures where cow bells tinkle all around and poinsettia trees blossom along the trails. There are two rice harvests a year, so chances are you might see farmers at work. Some of the best views are up on the ridge, where the **Khamsum Yuelley Namgyel Chorten** rises three floors high to protect the valley from the most common disasters, caused by wind, water or fire. The monks quarters climb up

Punakha Dzong

a wooded hillock and at the top is the cottage which serves as a royal retreat. Far below on the river bank is the spot where the Shabdrung threw stones to scare off the Tibetans, and sometimes one can watch local archers in the nearby meadows practising the national sport with makeshift bows and arrows. It is a long way from the serious contests in the capital, but there is still a victory dance when a player hit a bullseye and there may be a few ladies singing romance to encourage their team or telling rude jokes to distract opponents. It is all part of the tradition.

A four hour drive north of Punakha leads to **Gasa** ❾, the least populated district in Bhutan and home to the Laya community, numbering around 3,000 nomadic herders who trade yak products and medicinal herbs. The main sights are the Gasa Dzong where a festival is held in the spring and the hot springs beyond the end of the road. Remote villages such as Laya – which has the district's only guesthouse – and **Lunana**, tucked among the glaciers, are accessible only on trek. Much of Gasa is protected by the **Jigme Dorji National Park** ❿, which includes some of the highest peaks in the kingdom and over 100 glacial lakes. Takin, blue sheep and the elusive snow leopard are among the creatures who live in the park.

WANGDUE PHODRANG

From Punakha it is a short drive down the valley to **Wangdue Phodrang** ⓫, a small bazaar and district capital with a new town of its own called Bajo and a once magnificent dzong clinging to a ridge often buffeted by strong winds, high above the river. In June 2012 fire swept through the dzong, leaving little more than a shell, although locals managed to salvage some of the precious items. Rebuilding is expected to last until 2020 and a special permit is required to visit. Photos are not

Gangtey Gompa in the Phobjikha Valley

permitted at this stage. Beyond the town, the road continues above, then along, the valley, crossing the river Dang Chu at Tikke Zampa before tackling the long winding climb to the **Pele La pass** ⑫. At 3,420 metres (11,220ft) this is the main crossing point over the **Black Mountains** which divide Western and Central Bhutan.

About 3km (1.8 miles) before Pele La, a minor road turns off to the right towards the remote **Phobjikha Valley** ⑬, climbing to the Lawa La pass with sublime views of the peaks in good weather, wherever there is a clearing. Yaks often graze at the roadside – not as friendly as they look, so keep your distance. After the Lawa pass, slopes are covered in meadows and larch then at 2,900 metres (9,514ft) the broad Phobjikha valley spreads at your feet, a scattering of traditional farms with a few potato and turnip fields bordering the extensive wetlands.

On the edge of the Jigme Singye Wangchuck National Park, these are the wintering grounds of the rare black-necked cranes from the Tibetan plateau. Come November, their arrival is anxiously awaited in the valley, for should they fail to return, this would bring disaster. But the birds know their grounds, circling three times over Gangtey Gompa before they land. A special festival welcomes them with religious devotions, merrymaking and masked dancers who perform like the graceful birds. At the Visitors Centre managed by the RSPN (Royal Society for the Protection of Nature), powerful telescopes guarantee close-up views of the birds in season, but getting up before dawn can be rewarded with unforgettable sights as flocks of majestic cranes leave their roosting grounds in search of food. For an extra charge, local guides can take visitors to hides to watch the birds without disturbing them.

Cranes aside, 14 species of endangered birds have been spotted in the valley, among them the impressive imperial eagle, and there is plenty of wildlife in the surrounding forests, wild boar, barking and sambar deer, bears, leopards and thar, a Himalayan goat-antelope also known as 'serow'.

Nights are always cold in the valley, so be sure to pack warm gear, and expect snow in winter. The birds do not mind but monks and people move to gentler climes in Wangdue Phodrang. At the height of winter, the road is

Black-necked cranes

These tall elegant birds have a wingspan exceeding 2 metres (6.5ft) and weigh up to 5.5 kg (12lb). They are attracted to Phobjikha by the abundance of dwarf bamboo growing in the marshlands. They are highly respected by the Bhutanese and electricity cables are buried to ensure their safety. The birds return to Tibet around mid-February.

Buddha mural at Gangtey Gompa

often snowbound and in its splendid isolation, **Gangtey Gompa** sees very few visitors. The first temple was built by the grandson of the Nyingma saint Pema Lingpa and the gompa by the next reincarnation. An eight year restoration programme was completed in 2008. The work was done by skilled craftsmen helped by *gomchens*, or lay monks, who gave their labour for free. Besides the tower and main temple, famous for its paintings, statues and carvings, the complex includes meditation halls, living quarters for the monks and a Buddhist college while the gomchens' families are housed nearby.

CENTRAL BHUTAN

Central Bhutan has a lot to offer, from national parks rich in wildlife to bucolic valleys, cultural sites and unusual festivals. The strategic town of Trongsa sits on the edge of a dramatic gorge above the river Mangde, then over the Yutong La pass the highway drops down to the central valleys: Chumey, Choekhor, Tang and Ura, which together make up Bumthang. These are the kingdom's spiritual heartlands, studded with rivers and religious sites and shaped, they say, like a 'bumpa', a sacred bowl holding holy water. Others prefer to call it the land of beautiful girls, known as 'bum'. Sparse as it is, archaeological evidence points to prehistoric settlements in the south, which would make this region the oldest inhabited part of Bhutan.

TRONGSA

Beyond the Pele La pass, the road to Trongsa winds down through dwarf bamboo and firs followed by deciduous trees at lower altitude. There are rocks at the roadside, covered in religious paintings, and a couple of villages and farms scattered on the edge of the mustard fields. Sometimes visitors stop in Sephu, where locals weave bamboo mats and traditional baskets.

After the confluence of the Nikka and Nyala Chu rivers, the slow descent is framed by blue pines, rhododendrons and oaks until the **Chendebji chorten** ⓮ appears out of nowhere, inviting travellers to take a break in the cafeteria or picnic by the babbling

Chendebji chorten

stream. At 2,430 metres (7,972ft), it is a large multi-tiered structure, gleaming white, with the eyes of the Buddha looking in the four directions. Mirroring the Swayambhunath temple in Kathmandu, it was built by a Tibetan lama to subdue an evil spirit.

From there it is still 40km (24.8 miles) to **Trongsa** ⓯, down through the forest and up to a ridge, before reaching the Mangde Chu valley and heading north towards Trongsa through a dramatic landscape fringed in vertiginous drops. Later, you get the first tantalising view of Trongsa Dzong, suspended, it seems, between heaven and earth. Rising on a spur high above the gorge, it sends shivers down your spine the moment you see it, but this is just the start – the dzong will tease you for a long time, drifting in and out of sight until one

⊙ BAMBOO CRAFT

Alongside wood, bamboo has long been one of the most widespread skills in the Bhutanese cottage industry. With ample supplies, it provided domestic items from food containers and large carrying baskets to kitchen utensils, mats, ropes and fences, and was also used for archery and musical instruments. Skills were handed down through generations and children learned from an early age. But as modernisation steps in, it is more difficult to be patient, allowing the bamboo to dry for a year after cutting it before weaving it into shape. Then when the plant has flowered for two or three years, it simply dies. So today there are fewer plants and the younger generation are looking for faster and more lucrative ways of earning an income. Tourism, however, provides a welcome if limited outlet for beautifully finished products in plain natural colour or bright intricate patterns.

Trongsa Dzong

begins to wonder if it was all a dream. Stop at the viewpoint to take pictures, a magical place in winter when the wild cherry trees are in full bloom. But once again, the road is forced to turn off into a side valley and meander for another 14km (8.6 miles) before reaching Trongsa, an enticing town with neat whitewashed shops often kept by Tibetans, descendants of the refugees who came to Bhutan in the late 1950s.

The first temple was built by the Shabdrung's great-grandfather in 1543, then enclosed by the dzong in1644 to become the seat of the powerful rulers who, having asserted their authority over all others, established the monarchy in 1907. One can clearly see why Trongsa attained such importance. At 2,200 metres (7,217ft), in an impregnable location in the very centre of the kingdom, it controlled the east-west trading route with views extending for miles and a single trail which had to pass through the dzong, where gates could be

Golden langur in Trongsa

closed any time. On the mountainside above the fortress, the watchtower could promptly raise the alarm should there be any attack, and consequently, Trongsa strengthened its rule right across Central and Eastern Bhutan.

Built on several levels with red roofs and massive white walls closely hugging the contours of the ridge, backed by the mountains, **Trongsa Dzong** is one of the most hair-raising fortresses in the country and one can only marvel at the skill of architects and craftsmen. But there it is, a rambling maze of corridors, courtyards and stairs leading to 23 temples, filled with incense and flickering lights. On the site of the original temple, Chorten Lhakhang contains some stunning paintings and an impressive Buddha of the Future erected by the First King. The entrance to the tower depicts the paradise of Guru Rinpoche and there are paintings of Swayambhunath and the dzong in Punakha. The annual *tsechu* is held in December or January and anyone can join the locals who come to receive blessings, watch mask dances and the unfurling of the thongdrel, said to wash away all sins. Tashi Lebey, the farewell dance, brings everyone together in a moving finale.

Above the monastery, a path climbs up to the circular **Ta Dzong** (Mon–Fri winter 9am–1pm, 2–3.30pm, summer until 4.30pm, open Sat in peak season), the watchtower with four lookouts said to resemble a tiger, a lion, a mythical garuda and a dragon respectively. The tower is both a museum highlighting the history of Bhutan and a living place where one can worship at the shrines; hermits meditate in nearby retreats. Restored to celebrate the centenary of the monarchy, it is dedicated to the Wangchuck dynasty. The first two kings of Bhutan ruled from Trongsa in winter and the third, King Jigme Dorji Wangchuck, was born in Thruepang Palace (closed to visitors). As the ancestral home of the royal family, it is customary for the heir to the throne to serve as Trongsa Penlop before becoming king.

Attractions around Trongsa include **Kuenga Rabten**, a former royal residence roughly an hour's drive away through gentle countryside strewn with rice terraces and waterfalls.

The bridge entrance at Trongsa Dzong

The first floor was to store food, the second was for staff and soldiers and the third for royalty. A number of books from the National Library are kept in the palace and there is a temple with statues of Guru Rinpoche, the Shabdrung and the historical Buddha. A short walk up the hill is the **Karma Drubdey Buddhist Nunnery** which is usually open to visitors. Further down the valley is the **Eundu Palace**, a few minutes from the main road, the winter residence of the First King, with a chorten of Pema Lingpa, a display of weaponry and a chapel – closed to women – dedicated to the protective deities.

CHUMEY

Leaving Trongsa, the road climbs once again around dizzying bends – where one might catch a last glimpse of the dzong – before crossing farmland and woodland full of rhododendrons on the way to the Yutong La pass. At 3,400 metres (11,154ft), the pass is marked by multicoloured prayer flags and a chorten in the middle of the road. Blue pines stretch to the horizon but soon the forest comes to an abrupt end, as if cut by a giant knife, and Chumey, the first of the Bumthang valleys, opens out in front of you, sprinkled with monasteries, temples and villages where clay phalluses hang from the eaves and stones keep the roofs in place on windy days. Potatoes, barley and

Traditional hot stone bath

River stones heated on an open fire are dropped into a separate section in a wooden tub filled with cold water, releasing heat and health-giving minerals. More stones can be added if necessary to keep the water warm, with family members often following each other into the tub. The chance to experience this is available in some hotels and homestays.

Farmer in Bumthang

wheat are common crops, but king of the valley is buckwheat, which is used to make noodles and pancakes. There are willows and apple trees, sunflowers, haystacks raised on stilts drying in the sun, and here and there a traditional wooden bath steaming in a backyard.

On the edge of the fields, bells tinkle in two-storeyed prayer wheels and whitewashed mani stone walls bear witness to a pious land where Guru Rinpoche meditated and the saint Pema Lingpa discovered many of his sacred treasures.

The first temples appear as soon as you enter the valley. North of the river Chumey Chu near **Gyetsa**, the Nyingma **Buli Lhakhang**  has some stunning multi-sided pillars and Buddha images, while on the hill above, the **Tharpaling Gompa** was founded in the 14th century by Longchen Rabjampa, an exiled saint from Tibet. His statue can be seen in the temple alongside other saints. On the upper floor are paintings of the Amithaba heaven, or pure land of the Buddha. A rough 10km (6.2 miles) road climbs up to this monastery, which can also be reached by trekking from Jakar in the next valley. Higher still, at 3,800 metres (12,467ft), is **Choedrak** ❶, which contains a sacred spring, a Guru Rinpoche footprint and a stone skull said to be from a heavenly creature. Pilgrims who wish to be blessed by the God of Wealth continue to Zhambhala Lhakhang, the temple bearing his name.

South of the river, look out for **Domkhar Tashichoeling** ❿, the summer palace of the Second King. It's closed to visitors but you can peep into the courtyard. Then the road continues towards the quaint village of **Prakhar**, while a turning on the

⊙ YATHRAS

These are strips of wool, hand-spun and woven in bright geometric patterns, then stitched together into shawls, blankets, handbags, sweaters, coats or traditional clothes. The most expensive yathras are made from top quality Bhutanese wool and the cheaper ones from imported wool, but all are equally attractive. Yathras are specific to Bumthang, where girls learn from a young age to spin and work the loom, whatever their later ambitions. The greater the number of weavers in a family, the higher the status. Around a dozen villages are involved in the trade, some a day's walk from the road where they come to sell their work to dealers, for cash or household necessities. But beyond providing an income, weaving in Bumthang is part of the cultural heritage, preserving a skill practised almost exclusively by women. Zungney is a convenient stop to pick up a thing or two but most yathras make their way to Thimphu.

The dazzling setting for Bhutan's national highway, near Jakar

right heads south to **Nimalung Gompa** , home to 100 monks reputed for their musical talent. Across the river, the village of **Zungney** beckons with an eye-catching displays of yathras.

CHOEKHOR

After a short climb over the Kiki La pass, a modest 2,900 metres (9,514ft) by Bhutan standards, the idyllic Choekhor valley comes into view with lush Alpine meadows, fragrant hills draped in conifers and peaks glistening on the horizon. Along the river, scattered farms look like mountain chalets and indeed, they call this area 'little Switzerland'. There is even a real **Swiss Farm** making cheese, cider, apple brandy, honey and unfiltered Red Panda beer. **Jakar** ⑯ is the main settlement, a bustling trading post with a temple right in the town centre and a wide street lined with restaurants and shops, many of them rebuilt after extensive fires in 2010.

Jakar Dzong

Most visitors to the valley choose Jakar as a base where they will find a bank, a post office and a domestic airport operating flights to Paro and Gelephu on the southern border. On a ridge above the west bank of the river is **Jakar Dzong** , named after a white bird, which landed on this auspicious site in the 16th century, and accessed along a paved alleyway lined with marigolds and cypress trees. The current structure is said to be 1.5km (0.9 miles) in circumference and contains a traditional tower, courtyards and temples. There is a splendid panorama over the valley but for a bird's eye view of the dzong itself, continue up the hill to **Lamey Gompa** , a former monastery and royal residence, now occupied by the forestry commission, but worth a look for its finely decorated courtyard and colourful bamboo patterns woven under the eaves.

Back down to the river and up the valley are **Wangdichoeling Palace** , where the First King was born – see the giant prayer wheels just to the north – and **Chakhar Lhakhang ®** on the site of the once palatial 'iron castle', home to the troubled Indian king who sent for Guru Rinpoche.

Next comes **Jampey Lhakhang ®**, one of the oldest temples in the land built, like Kyichu in Paro, to subdue a demoness. A statue of Maitreya, the Buddha of the Future, is in the main sanctuary and paintings of the Thousand Buddhas line the circumambulation path. The temple to the right honours the Kalacakra deity representing the Wheel of Life and to the left the Guru Lhakhang is dedicated to the Rinpoche. But the highlight of the year in Jampey is the Drup, a five day festival when on a cold November night, men wearing nothing but masks pounce around a bonfire to perform the 'Naked Dance' to the hypnotic rhythm of cymbals and drums. It does not start until midnight but is worth the wait. There is much giggling from the local women, trying to identify their men, and some bewilderment among the tourists, as celebrations take place with unrestrained gusto and plenty of rather irreverent fun. They say that when an attempt was made to ban the daring dance, the valley was blighted by heavy rain and the dance reinstated. According to legend, it was invented by a holy man in the 14th century to tame the local demons.

North of Jampey, **Kurjey Lhakhang ℗** is one of the most important religious sites in the Choekhor valley, boasting a complex of three temples spanning over 300 years. Dating back to 1652, Guru Lhakhang is the oldest and holiest for it contains the meditation cave where Guru Rinpoche left a body imprint on a rock. The cave, however, is concealed by a massive statue of the Guru. Other images include the Past, Present and Future Buddhas, the Guru's disciples, Pema Lingpa and enlightened beings. On leaving the sanctuary, notice the garuda and snow lion under the eaves – both featured in Buddhist mythology – and the rock with a hole. Crawl through, say the Bhutanese, and all your sins will be taken away. The second temple, Sampa Lhundrup Lhakhang, was built by the Penlop of Trongsa, who later became the First Dragon King. It contains images of the Guardians of the Four Directions, local deities and a large statue of the Guru and his eight manifestations. The third temple was commissioned in 1984 by the Royal Grandmother, who also added the 108 chortens surrounding the complex. Offerings abound: fresh flowers, beautiful torma sculptures made of flour and butter, glowing butter lamps and ritual bowls of holy water.

Beyond Kurjey Lhakhang, an unmade road – soon to be black-topped – leads to Thangbi Gompa, but on a sunny morning, a walk through the countryside gives you the chance to breathe the fresh mountain air and meet a few locals along

Bridge near Kurjey Lhakhang

the way. There is much of interest: a rickety bridge draped in prayer flags; children in traditional dress on their way to school; a lama striding aof monks drying on a balcony; a farmer rushing to offer a rosy apple or a giant cucumber but expecting nothing in return. There are beehives on the edge of the fields and scare-crows with larger-than-life phalluses pointing to the sky. The river babbles

Fire and smoke ceremony at Thangbi Mani

over the stones, blue gentians and orchids line the trail and white-faced cows wander undisturbed around lonely shrines. The boxes scattered around are collection points for the milk to be delivered to Jakar.

Beyond the confluence of the Dhur and Chamkhar rivers, **Thangbi Gompa** Ⓤ displays terrifying deities and in the main sanctuary, statues of the Past, Present and Future Buddhas. On the upper floor are paintings of paradise and an image of the Buddha as a young prince. But this fairly isolated loca-tion claims one of the most exciting festivals in the valley. The Thangbi Mani is held in October when after the early morning rituals, glowing firewood is ceremoniously carried to an open field, where two haystacks are promptly set on fire. The crowds surge forward, running through the flames three times to purify their soul. Friends drag each other through, women hold on tight to their children, men pull up their collars to protect their hair. It is a mind-boggling sight and visitors soon step back as the heat rises. Fifteen minutes later, it is all over and everyone returns to the temple, jostling for space in the small courtyard. Masked dancers spin on the flagstones, chapattis are handed out and there are serious tales and naughty tricks before everyone queues up for the final blessing and heads home.

From Thangbi a rough road continues north for 10km (6.2 miles) to **Ngang Lhakhang**  though depending on time, one could walk along the river Chamkhar. Few visitors discover this remote temple built in the 15th century and now renovated. The name means 'temple of the swan' and among the images of holy men is Guru Rinpoche on a lotus flanked by swans. A festival is held around November-December, when local clans

Novice monks at Tamshing Gompa

perform traditional dances to honour the founding lama. The masks are kept in the upper sanctuary.

South of Thangbi on the eastern side of the valley, **Tamshing Gompa** ranks among the top Nyingma monasteries in Bhutan. It was constructed, they say, by Pema Lingpa himself with the help of female spirits, and has some unique features. Beyond the entrance, see the large prayer wheel in the especially built Mani Dungkhor temple and in the main building, the chapel inside the Assembly Hall where reincarnations of the saint, representing speech, body and mind, sit on their thrones during ceremonies. A barefoot Guru Rinpoche presides in the inner sanctuary flanked by the Present and Future Buddhas. See the Buddha of Long Life and display of dance masks in the upper chapel, which also holds a statue

of Pema Lingpa, sculpted by himself, though this not on show. Remarkable medieval paintings line the walls and there is a coat of mail made by Pema Lingpa. Carrying it three times around the shrine will purify the soul. It weighs 25kg (55lb). From Tamshing a trail leads back to Jakar but strong winds often sweep up from the south in the afternoon so be prepared for a chill in the air.

Meanwhile, for one day in February, highlanders gather in the upper valley to celebrate the Nomads Festival showcasing their unique culture. Visitors can

Small clay mouldings – called tsha-tsha – containing offerings at Membartsho

sit around the fire to feast on traditional recipes and the local brew; try on a Laya bamboo hat or a dress made of yak hair; watch a farmer grinding maize or tilling a field with an ox-drawn plough. There are also games including tug-of-war, song and dance and colourful pageantry once reserved for royalty. Festivities over, the herders head back to their tented camps, where they will soon begin preparations for the annual return to summer pastures.

TANG AND URA

About 11km (6.8 miles) from Jakar, a bumpy road heads north to the Tang valley, the domain of sheep and yaks at higher altitude. Shortly after the turn-off, a trail leads to the pilgrimage site of **Membartsho ⓧ**, the Burning Lake. There is no room for a temple but butter lamps and tiny urns containing the ashes of the dead highlight the sanctity of the site. As for the lake, it is more like a pool tucked in a gorge carved by the river Tang. Here, they say, Pema Lingpa had a vision of the Rinpoche's treasures lurking at the bottom of the lake and having recovered a chest, he returned with a large crowd and a burning lamp which only a miracle could keep alight, he proclaimed, as he jumped in naked. After a long time, he emerged with more treasures and the lamp still burning. So to this day people come here to pray and meditate, light incense sticks and feed the crows landing on the strangely-shaped rocks.

To the southeast is Ura, the highest of the Bumthang valleys. The road from Jakar follows the river Chamkhar, then climbs to the Ura La pass at 3,600 metres (11,811ft), looking out to **Gangkhar Puensum** in good weather, before descending to the traditional village of **Ura ❷**, dozing among highland meadows

◎ PEMA LINGPA

The saint was born in the Tang valley in 1450. Following a dream at the age of 25, he discovered the first of 34 treasures in the Burning Lake, thus becoming the most important 'terton' in a long line of treasure-hunting lamas. The treasures concealed by Guru Rinpoche were to be found over time by holy men as prophesied. Helped by female spirits, Pema Lingpa deciphered sacred scripts, created religious dances and discovered scrolls, relics and statues. His descendants built the Gangtey and Dramtse Nyingma monasteries while in the Tang valley, the **Kunzandrak Gompa ❼** was one of his residences, close to the hamlet where he was born. It contains three temples and a bodhisattva symbolising the Buddha's compassion, with 1,000 arms and 1,000 eyes. The gompa can be reached only on foot on a long arduous climb.

with its temple, cobbled lanes and tightly packed houses. Here women still wear sheepskins as waterproofs, which double up as blankets and cushions. The highlight of the year is the Yakchoe Festival, held in mid-spring, when dancers celebrate a special relic kept in the village. According to legend, it was left on the doorstep of an old woman who gave water to a lama and has been handed down through the family ever since. The August festival celebrates the Matsutake mushrooms found in the forests of Ura.

NATIONAL PARKS

In its privileged location at the heart of the kingdom, Central Bhutan is almost surrounded by national parks and sanctuaries, mostly interconnected as they spread across the country from ice fields in the north to jungle in the south.

To the north is the **Wangchuck Centennial Park** ⑰, the largest and the most recent, opened in 2008 to celebrate 100 years of the royal dynasty. From 2,500 to 5,100 metres (8,202 to 16,732ft), it consists mostly of blue pines and Alpine meadows and contains the headwaters of four main rivers. Wildlife includes takins, snow leopards, black bears and 100 species of birds. It is linked to the Jigme Dorji National Park in the west and the Bumdeling Wildlife Sanctuary in the east.

In the centre, covering much of the Trongsa district and spilling into neighbouring areas, the **Jigme Singye Wangchuck National Park** ⑱ rises from subtropical vegetation to chir pine, broad-leaved and conifer forests, meadows and snow. It protects the Black Mountains, claims 450 species of birds, resident and migratory, and is home to Himalayan bears, red pandas and tigers.

West of Sarpang along the southern border, the **Phibsoo Wildlife Sanctuary** ⑲ is a small strip of land protecting

Red panda in the trees

Bhutan's last natural sal forest – sal are briefly-flowering trees featured in Buddhist lore. Hornbills, spotted deer, elephants, tigers and gaur (the tallest species of wild cattle) are just a few of the creatures in this sanctuary, which is connected to the Jigme Singye Wangchuck and Royal Manas national parks.

Off-limit for years due to security problems on the Indian border, **Royal Manas** ⑳ has now reopened but tourism is still at an early stage, with few facilities and roads. It is the oldest protected area in Bhutan and is best visited between November and March, keeping clear of heavy monsoon rains. It harbours a rich variety of wildlife such as one-horned rhinos, clouded leopards, water buffaloes, Bengal tigers, elephants, gangetic dolphins and golden langurs covered in long, silky fur. It also has an abundance of plants, some used in religious ceremonies, others for nutrition and medication. It borders the Jigme Singye Wangchuck National Park to the north and to the south

Traditional medicine

Once known as 'the Land of Medicinal Herbs', Bhutan has incorporated the tradi-tional Tibetan-based medi-cine into its modern health system. Combined plants and minerals provide 300 treatments and are always the first option, often ac-companied by religious rituals, though serious illnesses are handled with western science.

the Manas National Park in Assam which is a World Heritage site. The park on the Bhutanese side is on the Unesco tentative list.

EASTERN BHUTAN

The 'People of the East', or Sharchops, once claimed the largest ethnic group in Bhutan. Today, Ngalops and Sharchops make up the Drukpa but the latter still speak their own language, as well as Dzongkha, and account for some of the country's most densely populated districts. However, one would hardly notice it beyond a few towns. Many live in remote valleys or deep in the hills where ethnic minorities – some numbering barely 1,000 – continue to survive with their own traditions and dialects. This is a land of mountains and rugged hills, fields and forests, deep gorges and steep slopes, arid in places due to the slash and burn agriculture practised in the past.

Having lagged behind Western Bhutan for a long time, the East is forging ahead, with new hotels and trekking trails, but it is still the least visited region and you are unlikely to meet a tour group. Yet for intrepid travellers, there is much to enjoy, unspoilt villages and wildlife sanctuaries, authentic homes-tays, sacred sites, Buddhist festivals or animist rituals. The domestic airport is currently closed but for those who have sufficient time, the lateral road will lead to new pastures right off the beaten track.

DRIVE TO LHUENTSE AND MONGAR

It is 190km (118 miles) from Jakar to Mongar and a seven hour drive on one of the most dramatic roads in Bhutan. Soon after Ura, the highway begins to climb through the **Phrumsengla National Park** ㉑, where ancient forests of chir pines and firs cling to precipitous ridges, their branches getting shorter as the altitude rises. From 700 to 4,400 metres (2,296 to 14,435ft) the park boasts a rich biodiversity, with mammals ranging from tigers to snow leopards and over 300 species of birds such as the endangered rufous-necked hornbill, the colourful satyr tragopan (crimson horned pheasant) or the beautiful nuthatch. In an effort to preserve the forest and maintain the balance between people and nature, villages are being provided with solar panels and corrugated galvanised iron roofs.

Driving in the snow at Thrumshingla Pass

Prayer flags at Trumshing La

At 3,780 metres (12,402ft), you reach **Trumshing La** ㉒, the second highest road pass in Bhutan and a lonely sort of place, brightened up by garlands of auspicious prayer flags and views of Gangkhar Puensum in clear weather.

On the other side is Eastern Bhutan, where a long precipitous descent requires all the luck one can get. After an hour or so, the forest gives way to the grassy slopes of the Sengor valley, a popular area for birdwatchers. Cows and sheep wander across the road but soon you are back in the wilds, with mountains stretching as far as the eye can see. Streams and waterfalls rush down the slopes, and above the dizzying drops, the road barely hangs from the cliff face on the long steep descent towards Yong Khola. Nestling in a side valley of the river Kuri Chu, the village appears like a mirage among banana plants, orange trees, bamboo and maize. Soon there are rice terraces, mango and papaya trees. Some 60km

(37 miles) from Sengor, the road reaches Kuri Zampa, having dropped over 3,000 metres (9,842ft) from the Trumshing La pass. A Nepali-style chorten stands by the bridge and it is now 25km (15.5 miles) to Mongar, past Gangola where a side road turns north to Lhuentse.

Few people visit **Lhuentse ㉓** – also known as Kurtoe – but it is one of the ancestral homes of the royal family and is reputed for its textiles, which are often considered the best in the country. In Khoma and other villages women can be seen on the doorsteps, working on backstrap looms where supplementary wefts produce the finest brocade on silk, known as kushuthara. These are expensive gifts, often commissioned for important guests, but during the lively three day *tsechu*, everyone can admire the beautiful attire worn for the occasion. Lhuentse has a picturesque dzong on a rocky outcrop with mountain views but expect unpaved tracks to the villages. Just 2km (1.2 miles) from the dzong is the village of

⊙ PRAYER FLAGS

Prayer flags are a common feature in Bhutan, thought to have originated in the Bon animist tradition. They are inscribed with mantras, or Buddhist prayers, and come in five colours, blue for the sky, white for air, red for fire, green for water and yellow for earth. Tall ones are usually planted on mountain passes or at the entrance to temples and sacred sites; small ones, known as wind horses, are hung like garlands on trees, bridges or houses. They bless the surroundings and spread goodwill and compassion across the world. They are treated with respect and when they need to be replaced, they should be burnt rather than discarded.

Gangzur, where women are encouraged to revive the old pottery skills. Above Dungkhar, 40km (24.8 miles) from Lhuentse, is the **Peak of Rinchen Bumpa**, a pilgrimage site where Guru Rinpoche meditated in a cave.

At 1,600 metres (5,249ft), **Mongar** ㉔ is set on a ridge and as capital of the district, it has its fair share of modern buildings. It is sometimes known as the 'Bastion of the Zhongarps', recalling the officials who once ruled from the old dzong, now a crumbling ruin still visible from the highway as it descends to Lingmenthang. Mongar has long been a trading centre and is a convenient overnight stop on the 11-hour journey from Jakar to Trashigang. Only a handful of tourists linger here but it is worth a stroll along the main street for the traditional shops and houses lining the way, the clock tower, the large prayer wheel one should spin for an auspicious day and the new dzong built in the 1930s on a gentle slope rather than a hilltop. A four day *tsechu* is held in November.

On the main street in Mongar

EAST TO TRASHIGANG

Leaving Mongar for Trashigang – a distance of 91km (56.5 miles) – the road climbs again through hemlock and pepper trees, accompanied by the constant whirring of crickets. Beyond the Kori

The Yadi Zigs

La pass at 2,400 metres (7,874ft), cows often graze at the roadside, their new-born calves blessed by wooden phalluses hanging from their necks. The descent is sure to bring an adrenalin rush as some bends require a three-point turn. Most testing are the Yadi Zigs, a series of hairpin switchbacks beyond the village by the same name. Bottle brush, flamboyant and orange trees mingle with potatoes and rice. In season guavas are sold at the roadside and the scent of lemon grass fills the air.

Crossing the bridge over the Sheri Chu at an altitude of just 700 metres (2,296ft), the road heads up over a ridge to reach the Drangme Chu valley, winding its way around until Thungdari where a head-spinning track zigzags up to **Drametse** ㉕ – 'the peak where there are no enemies' – and one of the main monasteries in Eastern Bhutan. It is only 18km (11 miles) in distance but it takes an hour to get there, 1,350

Lemongrass

In Eastern Bhutan lemongrass grows wild under the chir pines. It is a sustainable resource providing income for farmers. It is harvested by hand and the essential oil extracted for air sprays, soap, cosmetics and pharmaceutical products. The scent repels insects but for the Bhutanese, the natural fragrance is considered 'good for spirit, body and mind'.

metres (4,429ft) above the valley. The Gompa was founded in the 16th century by Choeten Zangmo, the great-granddaughter of Pema Lingpa. Her funerary chorten is in the main temple, guarded by statues of Guru Rinpoche and Pema Lingpa, the latter a mirror image sculpted by himself, according to legend. The upper floors are dedicated to protective and long life deities. Home to about 90 lay monks and ordained Nyingma monks – celibate or married – Drametse is the birthplace of the famous Drum Dance revealed in a vision, now performed in festivals across the country and listed as oral and intangible heritage by Unesco. The temple is closed for renovation until 2018, but there are stunning views over the gorge where the river carves its way below rose-coloured hills speckled with bushes and small trees. Tracks vanish into the distance, terraced fields struggle for space, squeezing on the edge of the water or climbing up the slopes, and the eerie silhouette of **Trashigang Dzong** 26 looms high on a spur, guarding the route as it has done for over 300 years.

Surrounded by ravines, rivers and mountain, it is an awesome sight and they say that when Tibetan invaders looked up at the 'dzong in the sky', they promptly turned back. Up there, monks quarters and civic offices share the only courtyard and there are several temples dedicated to religious masters, lamas and Guru Rinpoche. Paintings of the yeti attract much attention and there is a chapel dedicated to the fearsome Yama, god of death and guardian of the faith. During the *tsechu* held in late autumn, sacred dances are performed to appease the deity. The dzong is under renovation until 2018.

But when you approach the Chazam bridge flanked by a mythical snow lion, the town remains out of sight. Then having crossed the river, the road winds back around the hill and finally climbs up to Trashigang, the district capital tucked behind the promontory. A prayer wheel stands on a square lined with small bars and shops selling anything from buns and cakes to noodles and handicraft. There is often a vegetable market where you might spot the semi-nomadic Brokpa. They

Trashigang Dzong, overlooking the valley

Yeti

Known as *migoi*, meaning wild or strong man, the Bhutanese yeti of legend is descrived as being covered in hair, except for his face, which may be reddish, brown or black. The overpowering smell is his first line of defence but it is said that yetis can easily escape by becoming invisible and sometimes confusing followers with backward facing feet.

are herders from the Merak and Sakteng valleys, recognised by their yak-hair hats with braids hanging around the face to deflect the rain.

Trashigang, the 'Jewel of the East', may seem remote at first sight, but situated above the confluence of the Gamri Chu and the Drangme Chu – the main branch of the **Manas Chu** – and with roads heading east, west, north and south, it is a good base to explore the nearby villages and see traditional houses made of rammed earth, stone and timber. Cattle is kept on the lower floor, living quarters are upstairs – some still accessed by ladders hewn out of tree trunks – and there is usually an open-sided attic to dry the ubiquitous chillies. See the finely carved cornices above the timber-framed windows and the auspicious signs adding delicate pastel colours on the whitewashed walls. There are more decorations inside and shrines for daily offerings.

A popular excursion is to **Khaling** ㉗, 54km (33.5 miles) south of Trashigang. Beyond Sherubtse university college with its superb views from the hilltop, the road tackles the usual bends and the Yongphu La pass, then continues past the new Karma Thegsum Gompa to the bustling little town of Khaling. Visit the National Institute for the Visually Impaired, which has developed a Braille script for Dzongkha, and the National Handloom Development Centre, 3km (1.8 miles) out of town, where women from remote areas receive training before being contracted out to work in their own villages. Some come to the centre with a degree of experience handed down from their mothers, others have none, but working on backstrap looms, all learn to produce high quality fabric in a variety of colours and patterns.

Beyond Khaling the road continues towards Wanrong village, where women graze their sheep among daphne and edgeworthia bushes, then on through the **Pemagatshel** district with its rich farmland and forest and the scenic Yongla Gompa, built on a hill shaped like a sacred dagger. In clear weather the views are some of the best in the country, stretching from the Himalaya to the plain of India. From there it is still over two hours to the border crossing in **Samdrup Jongkhar**.

Local in his stilt house, Pemagatshel

In the far southeastern corner, the **Khaling Wildlife Sanctuary** ㉘ adjoins a similar reserve across the border. From 400 metres (1,312ft) to 2,200 metres (7,217ft), it harbours elephants, leopards, pygmy hogs and gaurs. It is the smallest protected area in Bhutan and is connected by biological corridors to the Royal Manas National Park and the **Sakteng Wildlife Sanctuary** ㉙ east of Trashigang.

Sakteng is sparsely inhabited by semi-nomadic tribes and with its wide range of habitats virtually untouched by development, it is on the Unesco tentative list. It is well known for rhododendrons, totalling 35 species out of the 46 found in Bhutan, and primulas, blue poppies, gentians and cordyceps fungi highly valued for their medicinal properties can be found. The sanctuary is home to Himalayan bears, musk and barking deer, and

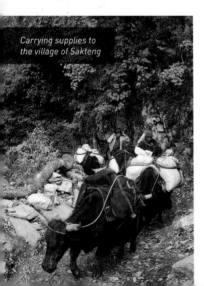

Carrying supplies to the village of Sakteng

locals have long reported sightings of the mythological yeti. The 146 species of birds include the Assamese macaw, blood pheasant, grey-headed woodpecker and rose finch.

Another worthwhile excursion takes you east of Trashigang – though not as far as Sakteng – along the river Gamri Chu then up to Rangjung, a pretty village with an ornate chorten and a monastery built in 1990, before climbing again through corn fields and rice terraces. At 1,570

Weaving a woollen yathra scarf the traditional way

metres (5,150ft), you reach **Radhi** ⓿, a quiet little place where maize dries under the eaves and women spin and weave on the doorstep. This area is famous for silk weaving – especially raw silk known as 'bura' – and visitors may be able to buy beautiful scarves and shawls in surrounding villages.

TRASHIYANGTSE

Beyond Trashigang the road heads north towards Trashiyangtse past **Gom Kora**, one of the most holy sites in the East. Sixty steps down from the road, under an enormous black rock, is the cave where Guru Rinpoche meditated and subdued a demon disguised as a snake. Across the river, farmers are busy harvesting rice, winnowing, carrying hay on their backs, but here it is all spinning wheels, offerings and prayer beads. Young monks have lessons on the grassy slope in good weather and Guru Rinpoche presides in the temple among relics and imprints, such as his foot, the hoof of his horse, the large egg of a garuda whose shape he had assumed and a fertility stone to be used with caution. Crawling through the cave is only for the 'pure', but 'sinners' can make a fresh start by climbing up, then running down the steep rock, though few would dare. Once a year at festival time, pilgrims circumambulate the rock and gompa throughout the night, a time when devotion and romance go hand in hand. Then the traditional East Bhutan courtship ritual of 'night hunting', an increasingly controversial practice – boy finds girl, creeping into her house in the darkness with or without prior arrangement, concluding with the couple engaged in the morning, theoretically – requires no effort at all.

Beyond the sleepy village of Duksum, the road continues to **Trashiyangtse** ㉛ along the river Kulong Chu, soon entering a precipitous gorge with overhanging rocks and barely a sprinkling of trees. A few hamlets are scattered high on the slopes or along the ridge then beyond the 'rock of 1,000 prayers', Trashiyangtse comes into view, 53km (32.9 miles) from Trashigang. It is a welcoming sight, a hidden valley where glistening roofs and terraced fields cascade down to the river, framed by wooded slopes. The new dzong on the hill has civilian offices, the old dzong by the river is reserved for the monks, a ramshackle building with lots of steps and ladders leading to temples dedicated to Guru Rinpoche, Buddha, the Shabdrung and the Gods of Compassion, Power and Knowledge; note that one of the chapels is reserved for men.

The most iconic sight in Trashiyangtse is **Chorten Kora**, a Nepali-style stupa built in the 18th century by Lama Ngawang Loday who, says the legend, brought back a model of Bodhnath temple in Kathmandu, carved in a radish which unfortunately shrivelled up during the journey. So this is not the perfect replica but nevertheless, nestling on the edge of the paddies by the glistening river, Chorten Kora is an inspiring place. Two festivals are held in late winter, one bringing pilgrims from all over Eastern Bhutan and the other from Arunachal Pradesh over the border to remember one of their own, an eight year old girl sacrificed long ago to appease a demon.

Another must-see is the **National Institute for Zorig Chusum** where talented students, like those in Thimphu, are given the chance to excel in some of the traditional arts and crafts. Trashiyangtse is especially reputed for wooden bowls and handmade paper. On graduation day which falls on the 15th day of the third month in the Bhutanese calendar, there are skill demonstrations, exhibitions and sales of finished products. Profit is ploughed back into the Institute. Visitors are

Chorten Kora

welcome any time but the centre is closed in July and for two months in winter. If you can't visit the Institute, head down to the river and you might spot a lone villager or two making paper in a meadow. Once used exclusively for religious texts, today's handmade paper is sold in every craft shop in Bhutan in a range of stationery or decorative items.

All around Trashiyangtse, hills and vales are sprinkled with holy sites. A 45 minute walk from Womanang school is **Dechen Phodrang**, a rarely visited place on the bank of a rushing stream, protected by a giant cypress tree. According to legend, this was Guru Rinpoche's banner. The temple built into the rock contains a sacred spring and a Guru's imprint, with many more scattered in the surrounding area. Other religious sites accessed only on foot include the remote **Omba Ney**, often

Men making paper in Trashiyangtse

called the Tiger's Lair of the East, and **Rigsum Gompa**, the Temple of the Three Gods perched high on a slope above a forest ablaze with rhododendrons in the spring. When it was renovated in 2000 it took three months and 10 artists to paint the interior. The temple is dedicated to the Gods of Compassion, Power and Knowledge and includes 108 prayer books, wrapped in red and gold cloth, and paintings of the Medicine Buddha and a Green Tara, both holding healing plants.

> ### Handmade paper
>
> Daphne plants produce strong paper, while edgeworthia produces softer, whiter paper. The bark is stripped from the plants, pounded into pulp and soaked, then a bamboo screen is dipped into the mixture until covered by a thin layer. Screens are hung to dry in the sun. The whole process takes up to three days.

A 40 minute drive north of Trashiyangtse, the **Bumdeling Wildlife Sanctuary** ㉜ is on the Unesco tentative list for maintaining harmony between the traditional culture and natural world, protecting diverse ecosystems which include bamboo, broad-leaved forests, pines and Alpine pastures. It is home to snow leopards, red pandas, capped langurs and tigers, and the sanctuary also provides wintering grounds for the black-necked cranes from Tibet, though in smaller numbers than Phobjikha. Over 400 species of birds have been recorded and 130 species of butterfly, including the endemic swallowtail, named Ludlow's Bhutan Glory, after the British botanist who discovered it; it is now regarded as the national butterfly. The protected Himalayan yew and blue poppy are found in the sanctuary, which also claims over 40 species of wild orchids. From Trashiyangtse, the sanctuary extends into the Lhuentse and Mongar districts.

Participants at Wangdue festival

WHAT TO DO

Bhutan has more to offer than cultural sites. Shopping for arts and crafts; wellness for body and mind; and outdoor activities from gentle treks to adventurous sports – visitors will always find plenty to do, whether travelling alone, with a group or as a family. Trips can be arranged to cater to special interests, such as wildlife, textiles or children's activities, but this should be requested at the time of booking. Depending on personal choice and operator, you may be able to join a group or plan a tailor-made trip as a solo traveller or couple.

SHOPPING

Arts and crafts are deeply ingrained in Bhutanese culture, where creating beautiful things is often regarded as a pious act, earning merits by preserving unique long-standing traditions. Authentic Bhutanese crafts are handmade, requiring days or even months of work, so prices are high and any attempt to bargain would show a lack of appreciation, though the Bhutanese would be far too courteous to point this out.

In Thimphu, where you will find the widest choice, check out the **National Handicrafts Emporium**, **Zorig Chusum** and smaller outlets along Norzin Lam, and in Paro, **Chencho Handicrafts** by the town square. Some items may be cheaper in Bumthang, where there are fewer tourists; although you cannot always buy direct from villagers, some small manufacturers may sell items.

TEXTILES

If you purchase only one thing, this is what it should be. The best comes from Central and Eastern Bhutan. Cotton, the

Imported crafts

Crafts imported from India or Nepal are available in markets and some shops, cheaper than genuine local items, and bargaining is accepted on these. Guides are not on commission and will always give you an honest answer regarding the origin of the product. Be aware that buying or exporting antiques is illegal.

cheapest, is used in traditional dress and smaller items; wool is for beautiful handwoven *yathras* in Bumthang, warm yak-hair jackets and ethnic hats. Silk, the most stunning, is displayed in festive *kiras* and *ghos* (women and men's national dress respectively). A national dress may not be suitable back home but the blouse and jacket make fabulous party wear while a length of Bhutanese fabric can be used as a wall hanging, bedspread or table runner. Shawls, belts, purses and bags are ideal souvenirs: colourful, useful and easy to carry.

JEWELLERY AND RELIGIOUS ARTICLES

Silver is popular mostly in necklaces, earrings and the finely embossed shoulder clasps fastening the kiras. Ethnic jewellery is distinguished by coral and turquoise worn with silver or gold. Of special interest are dzi stones, the real ones made of natural agate, sold in amulets, necklaces and bracelets. Called 'heavenly pearls', they are believed to enhance spirituality and bring positive vibes.

Religious articles include prayer wheels and flags, temple bells, singing bowls, Tibetan cymbals and small Buddha statues. Those may come from India or Nepal, but the most genuine article is likely to be a *thangka*, a religious banner painted according to tradition, most expensive if mounted on brocade and costing anything from $30 to over $1,500. Painted masks, made of wood or papier-mâché, are also on sale, representing earth-bound creatures or the gods featured in sacred dances.

BAMBOO, BOWLS AND SUNDRIES

Cane and bamboo are exquisite souvenirs, affordable, unbreakable and light. They come in all shapes and sizes, as table mats, Laya hats or baskets, like the clever 'banchung' made from two tightly-fitting parts, designed to carry food, then be used as plates. The highly prized bowls and cups from Trashiyangtse are made of special wooden knots; from the eastern reaches come the decorated wooden wine containers crafted in the small village of Khenghar.

Weaving a woollen yathra blanket

Locals bathing in Gasa tshachu (hot springs)

Other items to look for are Bhutanese stamps, handmade paper, incense sticks and local music, both religious and secular. Then, in case you would like to put your feet up during your travels, browse one of Thimphu's bookstores, such as **DSB** near the Druk Hotel or **Kuenjung Enterprises** in the Khamsa complex, and pick up one of the lovely books on Bhutan. You will not find a better selection anywhere else.

WELLNESS

HOT SPRINGS

'*Tshachus*' have long been popular with the locals and visitors are beginning to follow suit. The best known springs are in **Gasa** – where camping is the only option – in the Jigme Dorji National Park. It only takes 45 minutes to travel the road accessing it, but anyone who would like time to meditate in awesome scenery can opt for a six hour trek from Damji village through pine and oak-covered hills, accompanied by tumbling streams and views of the peaks. The communal baths have different temperatures and healing properties and if you are lucky, you might even spot some of the wildlife, even a few takins, coming for a drink in their own pool.

Other venues include **Chubu Tshachu** –the 'sacred spring' in the Punakha district – **Dhur Tshachu** in Bumthang near the village by the same name and **Duengmang Tshachu** by the river Mangde, where you are likely to encounter members of the local tribe. In **Gelephu** down south, a soak in the hot springs can be complemented by a traditional hot stone bath.

MEDITATION

In the beautiful scenery of Bhutan, it is easy to meditate and there are a number of retreats led by spiritual leaders around the country, usually near monastic schools, temples or monasteries. Visitors may come for a day and a few hours silent meditation in the hills, or for a week long retreat that will include prayers, religious rituals and connecting with the local community.

Climbing to Taktsang in the Paro valley is truly

Meditation retreats are popular in Bhutan

inspiring but for those who prefer to relax in comfort, some hotels feature yoga or meditation when sessions may end with the healing sound of an Himalayan singing bowl. Traditional herbs and hot stone baths may also be available, alongside massage, body wraps, such as honey and milk, or a red rice and lemon grass polish. To avoid disappointment, let your operator know what you would like when you book, whether it is a single session or a themed trip.

OUTDOOR ACTIVITIES

The same applies to outdoor activities, however short. All requests, whether for a half-day trek, an archery tournament or birdwatching for a day, rafting or a trip to a botanical garden,

Trekkers with their guide in Thimphu

should be made to your guide or operator in advance. Last minute arrangements are often difficult and less likely to succeed.

But even when everything has been carefully planned, it is always best to be prepared for the unexpected. A trek could be re-routed due to adverse weather, minor

A peak too high

Note that climbing mountains over 6,000 metres (19,685ft) is prohibited for both safety and religious reasons. Gangkhar Puensum claims to be the highest unclimbed peak in the world.

roads may be snowbound in winter, and landslides and road works can cause delays any time on the highway, so you may miss an activity. Accept changes with good grace: anger leads nowhere and is not the Bhutanese way of doing things.

TREKKING

Bearing in mind the altitude and mountainous terrain, a trek labelled 'gentle' may feel demanding to less seasoned walkers, especially on a first visit to the Himalaya. Nevertheless, there are options to suit different levels of fitness and available time. Equipment is provided, though you may need to bring a sleeping bag, there will be pack animals to carry luggage and guides and cooks to look after you. The best times to trek are mid-October–November, when clear skies are more likely, or spring if you wish to see the rhododendrons.

Easier treks include the 3 day **cultural trek** in Bumthang, taking in villages and temples – maximum ascent 750 metres (2,460ft) – and the 2 day **Punakha trek** – also possible in winter – tackling relatively gentle slopes along the old trail from Thimphu. The **Druk Path** – 6 days – leads from Paro to Thimphu across a wild area dotted with blue pines and lakes up to an altitude of 4,206 metres (13,799ft). In the east, the 7 day **Merak Sakteng** is a moderate hike through semi-nomadic lands and the wildlife sanctuary

More demanding is the 9 day **Jomolhari trek** reaching 4,930 metres (16,174ft) but weather permitting, the views of Bhutan's second highest peak from the base camp are second to none. The Laya-Gasa trek follows the Jomolhari for the first five days then continues through pristine landscape. But most challenging of all is the 25 day **Snowman**, heading to the Lunana district then across to Central Bhutan. The highest point is 5,320 metres (17,454ft) and only the most resilient manage to complete what many regard as one of the world's hardest treks.

FLORA AND FAUNA

Besides the challenging hikes, full or half-day walks reward visitors with wonderful scenery and possibly wildlife sightings. In Thimphu, see the **Motithang Takin Preserve**, then wander around the **Botanical Garden** in Serbithang, 15km (9 miles) from town, inaugurated in 1999 to celebrate the Fourth King's Silver Jubilee. This is not about neat flower beds and lawns but native and exotic trees, shrubs and herbs, orchids and fabulous rhododendrons. With its bamboo garden and water features, it is a favourite picnic spot for city-dwellers at the weekend, but is always peaceful with scenic views from the hilltop.

A short drive from the Dochu La pass, the **Royal Botanical Park** boasts a popular Botanical Garden where rhododendrons splash myriad colours in the spring. Visitors can wander along the trails ranging from 1km (0.6 mile) to 4.7km (2.9 miles), through a cool moist forest of oak, magnolia and birch. There is a small lake, a pagoda where locals leave offerings and an information centre. The Royal Botanical Park is connected to

Bhutan is home to many birds, including the great hornbill

the **Jigme Dorji National Park** and for those who venture on longer trails, sightings may include musk deer, red panda, blood pheasant or the beautiful Himalayan specimen, known as Monal, which displays all the colours of the rainbow.

Bears and other large creatures hide deep in the forest, at least during the day, but wherever you are in Bhutan, from Paro to Punakha or Trashiyangtse, you are sure to see at least a few of the 670 species of birds recorded to date. Keen bird-watchers can book a specialised week-long tour.

A typical birding tour would start near the Indian border then make its way across Bhutan with sightings of resident, migratory and endangered species, as diverse as the habitats. Expect long drives, some walking, hotel and camp stays and services of expert guides. Budget packages are available in low season while some of the more expensive tours include bird photography.

For enthusiasts of the big game lurking in the subtropical south, the **Royal Manas National Park** can arrange rafting, elephant and jeep safaris. Adventure is guaranteed but sadly sightings are not.

SPORTS

Adventure or gentle sport, join in or watch, there is something for everyone.

Adventure sports are relatively new but the country is catching up fast. Gaining popularity with Bhutanese and tourists alike is mountain biking, a more intimate encounter with the landscape than driving, but covering longer distances than one could on foot. Trails are suitable for most kinds of frames, whether on paved roads, dirt tracks or other rough terrain. Itineraries take in small towns and rural villages while more experienced riders can tackle challenging climbs up to 3,400 metres (11,154ft). Safety is paramount and a van follows the riders.

With its crystal-clear rivers tumbling from high valleys down to the plains, Bhutan offers rafting and kayaking opportunities. The best times are March–April and November–December, with options ranging from beginner to advanced courses, all with fully trained guides. The Paro

Mountain biking is gaining in popularity

Chu and the Upper Po Chu, the male Punakha river, are rated III-IV for difficulty, with 3 and 2 hour trips respectively; kayaking is also possible on the Po Chu. The Upper Mangde Chu in the Trongsa district is classed IV while the 5–7 hour trip on the Mo Chu (Punakha, class V, kayaks only) takes in the Tashitang's Devil Gorge.

> ### Rock climbing
>
> If you are into rock climbing, you could tackle one of the 13 bolted routes up 'The Nose' outside Thimphu. Ask your guide to arrange this through the Vertical Bhutan Climbing Club.

Bhutan is barely emerging as a golfing nation and at the moment only the 9-hole **Royal Thimphu Golf Course** is open to the public. At 2,500 metres (8,200ft) on the edge of town, it is not the most manicured in the world, but it is surprisingly challenging and where else would you tee-off with views of the snow-capped Himalaya and one of the most impressive dzongs in Bhutan? Even if you do not play, ask your guide if you could have lunch in the restaurant.

Other sporting options are more or less limited to joining the locals playing khuru in an open field as they throw heavy wooden darts to hit a target 10 to 20 metres away (33 to 66ft), or digor, using flat stones in an original version of the French game of pétanque. Of course one could always kick a ball with the kids, play badminton with the monks in a temple courtyard or volunteer for a strong man contest or a tug-of-war at festival time.

ENTERTAINMENT

A visit to Bhutan means busy days and quiet evenings across much of the country so if nightlife is a must, one should make the most of it in Thimphu. Whether in bars, clubs or outdoor venues, everyone is welcome and solo travellers and couples will soon be drawn into the crowd and make friends.

Mojo Park, the coolest bar in Thimphu, has live music, a magnet for the local youths dancing in kiras and ghos to the sound of Bhutanese pop or Indian metal. **Clock Tower Square** puts on traditional shows and the occasional rock concert. Some hotels stage cultural shows on a regular basis, or your guide could put in a request if you are travelling with a group. Then, if you are curious about the burgeoning film industry encouraged by the government, you could watch a Bhutanese movie (some are subtitled) in the **City Mall theatre**.

Otherwise, evening entertainment is mostly in the bars, livened up by Druk beer or a few swigs of *ara*, the local fire water, though officially Tuesday is a dry day right across the country. Karaoke is a popular pastime, since all Bhutanese learn

⊘ SPECTATOR SPORTS

Archery, the national sport, is exciting to watch, steeped in ancient religious rituals. Neither monks nor women are allowed to play. Visitors who are into football, basketball or cricket may be able to watch a game in Thimphu's Changlimithang stadium, which also hosts special events and celebrations. Anyone who visits Bhutan early September should look out for the Tour of the Dragon, a gruelling one-day cycling race, covering 268km (166 miles) over 4 mountain passes, from Bumthang to Thimphu. The race begins at 2am, ending between 6 and 7pm. There is also a yearly Marathon which raises funds for the Bhutan's Youth and Olympic Sports programmes.

to sing and dance from an early age. Songs can be in Dzongkha, Nepali or Hindi, but there may be a couple of English titles for the visitors' benefit. Drakyang bars have a slightly more racy version with young women tipped by a generally male audience to sing and dance. To be clear, the ladies remain fully dressed throughout and the entertainment is high quality. Card and 'carom' games are available in

Archery is the national sport

some bars. Carom is a kind of mini-snooker played on a board by flicking counters into the corner pockets.

Popular hang-outs in Thimphu include the **Om Pub** in Jo Jo's shopping centre, aimed at young professionals, the lively **Club Ace** on Phenday Lam with thumping electronic music and **Space 34** on Chang Lam which attracts people of all ages with dining, dancing and live music in the 'Divine Madman's Corner'.

All towns have bars and some may have a disco of sorts, often closing early but the party may go on elsewhere. Make friends and you might get invited.

CHILDREN

Children under five travel free then enjoy a 50 percent discount until they reach 11, a bonus for any family keen to share the experience. There are no specifically designed activities, apart from a few playgrounds, but children are warmly welcome and the best ice-breakers anyone could wish for. Avoid long drives or packing too much into a day, give them time to relax and make contact with local children, many of them speak at least a few words of English.

Take it a step further and ask if you could visit a school, a rewarding experience for the whole family and a chance to communicate and participate, perhaps with an impromptu English lesson or a singsong. Short homestays are also ideal for families, especially on a farm where one can help feed the animals, learn to play a few notes on a Bhutanese lute or draw pictures with the hosts.

Young ones love picnicking by a babbling river or riding a pony to the halfway point in Taktsang. Rafting – life-jackets provided – is usually suitable on the gentler stretches of the Mo Chu, the female river in Punakha, and most walks along the valleys are easy, filled with wide-eyed excitement when you have to cross a suspension bridge.

Ride elephants in the south, if the children can cope with the heat and possibly leeches, and in Thimphu take them to the Takin Preserve or for a treat, let them splash about in the public swimming pool.

Family life in Haa

FESTIVALS

Festivals brighten up the scene year round across Bhutan so timing a visit to take in a celebration should not be difficult.

Note that dates vary according to the Bhutanese calendar so months indicated below are approximate. Check with your operator before booking.

Photography is permitted during the festivals, except inside the temples or if the royal family are in attendance.

Be discreet during devotions, be as daring as you want with the jesters, but expect likewise in return, and if you would like a close-up picture of someone, ask with a smile and it will be granted.

February: Bumthang, Nomads Festival.
February/March: Punakha, Dromchen and Tsechu. Trashiyangtse, Chorten Kora.
March/April: Gasa Festival. Trashigang, Gom Kora. Paro Tsechu.
April/May: Lamperi, Rhododendron Festival. Bumthang, Ura Yakchoe.
June/July: Bumthang, Nimalung Tsechu. Bumthang, Kurjey Tsechu.
July: Haa, Alpine Festival.
August: Bumthang, Ura, Matsutake Mushroom Festival.
September/October: Haa Tsechu. Thimphu, Dromchen and Tsechu. Bumthang, Thamshingphala Choepa. Wangdue Phodrang, Tsechu.
October: Gangtey Tsechu. Bumthang, Thangbi Mani Festival.
October/November: Bumthang, Jakar Festival.
November: Phobjikha, Crane Festival. Bumthang, Jampey Lhakhang Drup. Bumthang, Prakhar Festival.
November/December: Bumthang, Ngang Bi Rabney. Mongar Tsechu. Trashigang Festival.
December: Nalakhar Festival.
December/January: Trongsa Tsechu. Lhuentse Tsechu.

EATING OUT

Bhutan is not a gourmet destination but with its own sizzling specialities combined with elements of Tibetan, Indian and Nepali cuisine, the food is exciting. Package tours are all inclusive, featuring breakfast and buffet dinner in the hotel, usually a mix of international and Asian cuisine, plus lunch in a local restaurant or from a picnic box depending on the itinerary. But that does not mean you cannot venture out of your comfort zone and try a local restaurant, or stop for a snack along the way.

TRADITIONAL FOOD

Bhutan's cuisine is unsophisticated, based on fresh organic produce cooked by simple methods: steam, stew or fry. It is generally less oily than Indian or Chinese fare, but slightly more tangy than Tibetan food. Local menus tend to be limited to a few choices, not necessarily all available, but everything is hot and tasty and worth the wait. Chillies are omnipresent while spices are sparsely used, except in the south, the most common being cardamom, ginger, caraway, garlic and curry. Every dish is served with a mountain of rice, as generously topped up as needs be, and if you do opt for curry, it may come white, without turmeric to add colour.

Meat and sometimes fish appear on the menu but

Roadside stalls

You will find them wherever you go: ladies sitting on the verge or smiling under makeshift shelters. They sell fresh curd and yak cheese, home-grown vegetables and cherry tomatoes bursting with flavour. Best of all is the fruit: apples, plums, guavas, avocados and oranges, depending on the region and season.

these are mostly imported, since for religious reasons, the Bhutanese do not kill. They might, however, eat meat as a treat on special occasions, while for herders in the remote highlands, yak meat, sweet and juicy or dried, provides an essential source of low-fat protein.

Fresh chillies for sale

National dish

Chillies and cheese sauce are everyone's favourites, put them together and you have Bhutan's national dish, *ema datshi*, as hot as you can bear it. 'Ema' are the chillies, red or green but equally fiery; datshi is soft melted cheese made from cow's milk curd, once the fat has been removed to make butter. It is delicious in a sauce but never eaten raw. No Bhutanese meal is complete without chillies and rather than seasoning, they are regarded as vegetables in their own right. Except of course for visitors, who may request them on a side plate just in case. Chillies and rice are accompanied by two or more side dishes, meat or vegetables, depending on availability and occasion.

Vegetables

Large tracts of agricultural land are found in the lower and mid-altitude regions, so vegetables are plentiful. This does not necessarily mean chefs can ring the changes since most dishes depend on the availability of fresh produce. It might be courgettes

every day or pumpkin if that is the season. Then there are turnips, radishes, spinach, onions, green beans and asparagus alongside the more intriguing fiddlehead ferns, nettles, orchids and river weeds which are collected in the wild. The forests also yield bamboo, yams, taro, sweet potatoes and banana flower buds. All are packed with vitamins and iron, tasty and exciting for adventurous vegetarians or indeed any food lover. For those who appreciate the thick velvety cheese sauce but not the chillies, this can also be served with potatoes or mushrooms, of which there are over 400 varieties. Matsutake mushrooms from the Ura valley are highly prized.

A Bhutanese plate of mixed vegetable dishes and rice

Rice

Except in areas where the soil favours maize or millet, and in Bumthang where buckwheat noodles and pancakes are the staples, rice is as essential as chillies in a Bhutanese meal. A farmer can eat up to 1kg (over 2lb) a day. It adds consistency to the meal, soaks up the heat from the chillies and makes cutlery redundant – although this is commonly used in towns and always provided for foreign guests. Otherwise, shape the rice into a ball, whether it is the white or red variety, and use it to scoop up the food. Always use the right hand as is customary in Asia.

Mix and match

The second most popular dish is *phaksha paa*, strips of pork, fresh or dried, sometimes mostly fat which is considered a delicacy, stewed with turnips or radishes and chilli powder, then topped with dried pork, green chilli strips and served with rice. Alternatively it can be accompanied by buckwheat dumplings stuffed with vegetables and melted cheese.

Many restaurants in Thimphu claim the best dumplings – Tibetan momos – but the Bhutanese often save this as a treat for special occasions. Dumplings can be filled with green vegetables, cheese, beef or pork. Other Tibetan specials include meat patties and noodle soup.

Jasha maru is a spicy chicken dish, minced or diced, served with tomatoes, vegetables and rice; *zow shungo* is rice with leftover vegetables, a sort of Bhutanese bubble and squeak. Tripe, they say, go down really well with plenty of chillies while soups and stews are most satisfying in winter, but look out for

⊙ RED RICE

Red rice – actually pinkish in colour – is Bhutan's culinary superstar, a whole-grain variety grown in the fertile Paro valley which is irrigated by mineral rich waters from ancient glaciers. It is quick to cook and feels light and slightly sticky when ready. Filling and healthier than white rice, it provides 80 percent of the daily requirements for manganese and 20 percent for phosphorus. It is also an antioxidant, rich in fibre and has a discreetly nutty flavour. It is the most delectable complement to any Bhutanese dish but is said to go particularly well with mushrooms and chillies. It can be served with a main course or as a steamed pudding.

small bones lurking among the veg. *Dal bhat* is steamed rice with lentil sauce, a Nepali staple popular in the south.

DESSERTS, DRINKS AND DOMA

Desserts

Anyone with a sweet tooth should be aware that dessert is merely an add-on to please hotel guests. Expect little more than a thin caramel or chocolate mousse, a bland jelly or rice pudding, but fruit is plentiful and fresh ice-cold cubes of watermelon are the finest antidote to hot chillies.

However, Paro and Thimphu have excellent bakeries and sweet cravings can soon be satisfied with a slice of apple pie or walnut cake, an éclair or a cream puff. Seasonal fruit can be bought in the markets while out in the country – almost every farm has a small orchard and there are plenty of wild berries and nuts.

⊘ HOME COOKING

As elsewhere around the world, home cooking is often best so consider a homestay for a night or two. With ingredients straight from the farm or the morning market, freshly cooked by your host, dinner will include a wide variety of dishes such as noodles, rice, fried potatoes, seasonal vegetables, dried beef and yogurt, served all at once in wooden bowls. This is both a taster meal and a banquet but before you tuck in, show your appreciation and do as the Bhutanese do, cover your mouth and say 'meshu meshu' (no, thank you), then accept with a smile when it is offered a second time. No need to worry, it will come.

For a really sweet treat, popular in western districts, try *Ngathrek Golop Lhakpa*, a variant of candyfloss flavoured with slightly salted butter tea and, as you would expect, a sprinkling of flaked chilli. It is best eaten with slices of apple, berries or yogurt.

Drinks

Tea with milk and sugar is the most popular drink, prepared for family, guests or visiting monks ready to

Monk preparing tea

perform a ritual. At festival time, everyone takes huge flasks of tea to the monastery to share with family and friends. *Tshringma* is a herbal tea named after the goddess of longevity; *sudja* is the Tibetan-style tea with yak butter and salt, more like a soup than a drink and a fine way to warm up on a frosty Himalayan morning.

Coffee is instant except in top hotels and a few cafés or restaurants, mostly in Thimphu and Paro. Soft drinks are widely available and safe, but the Bhutanese are not adverse to alcohol. Red Panda is an unfiltered beer produced in Bumthang and there is Druk, labelled red for beer or blue for lager. Chang is a beer-like drink while *ara*, a spirit made from rice or other grains, guarantees to set your throat on fire with at least 20 percent alcohol. Legally produced at home – as long as it is for private use – it is used in religious offerings and sometimes carried as a snake repellent. However it is often abused in rural areas, namely in Central and Eastern Bhutan.

Enjoying a picnic in Merak

Doma and more

No authentic Bhutanese meal is over until *doma* has been passed around. This is the famous betel nut mixed with lime powder, wrapped in a betel leaf and chewed. It is bitter-sweet, stains your teeth and lips red and is gently intoxicating.

But *doma* cannot beat yak cheese cubes for chewiness, hanging on a piece of string at roadside stalls and as hard as rocks. Pop one into your mouth and it will be with you all day. Even the slithers of dried yak skin served as appetisers are easier to swallow.

PICNIC, TREK AND COOK

Picnics are a pleasure and sometimes a necessity on long journeys. They come in two ways, local and tourist. Locals will prepare a traditional meal, packing the different dishes in bamboo or metal containers. Tourists get bland sandwiches on white bread, fruit, a bun and a carton of juice. Alternatively, you could shop for whatever you fancy in a supermarket before setting off.

Trekking is different with three hot meals a day prepared by the cooks. Expect fresh produce for the first few days then tinned food, all carried by ponies or yaks. A special treat on a trek may be a Bhutanese pizza, called Mengay, prepared with mashed rice, mushrooms, spring onions and whatever else is around. Feel free to watch how it is made and you might get a chance to help.

There are no regular cookery courses in Bhutan but anything can be requested at the time of booking. Plans will be made, then things might work out or might not. Just go with the flow. The most reliable venue may be the **Terma Linca Resort and Spa** in Thimphu but the one-hour cooking class led by hotel chefs could set you back $100.

MENU READER

Phrases below are in Roman script Dzongkha. Spellings can vary.

ara local spirit /whisky	**gongdo** egg
cha tea	**kewa** potatoes
chang beer	**meto kopi** cauliflower
chu water	**öndo** turnip
banda kopi cabbage	**sha** meat
bja sha chicken	**shamu** mushroom
datshi cheese	**thukpa** noodle soup
êma chillies	**tshöse** vegetables
gäza corn/maize	**tsoem** curry

USEFUL PHRASES

Where is... **gâti mo**
A restaurant **zakha**
A bar **changkha**
Are you serving food now **chö dato to za wigang ina?**
I don't eat meat **nga sha miza**
I don't like chillies **nga zhêgo êma dacikha miga**
This is too spicy **di khatshi dû**
This is enough **digi lâm mä**
Delicious **di zim mä**
Thank you **kadinchey**
May I have the bill **ga de chi mo**

PLACES TO EAT

Note that beyond the western cities and Jakar, hotels are usually the best and sometimes the only option for lunch or dinner. Meals are included in local and standard tourist restaurants and hotels – drinks may be extra – but if you choose your own restaurant, check if this will be covered by the agent. Confirm opening hours with your guide, who can reserve a table if you wish. Expect to be charged in luxury venues. Some top hotels include full or half- board, others, such as the Taj Tashi, breakfast only.

We have used the following symbols to give an idea of the price for a main course –should you need to pay– and a drink for one person in a restaurant or for a light meal and a drink in a trendy coffee-shop. Western-style three course dining with wine is available in top hotels.

$$$ over US$25
$$ US$12–25
$ below US$12

WESTERN BHUTAN

Paro

Brioche Café $$ *Tshongdue, Paro.* The best bakery in Paro, a brilliant place to indulge cravings for sweet treats and coffee. It will tickle your taste buds the moment you walk in, with cheesecake, plum, walnut or chocolate tart, croissants, and homemade ice-cream, including unusual flavours such as ginger and cinnamon. Also serves iced tea and decent sandwiches and given sufficient notice, they might even bake you a delicious birthday cake.

Bukhari at Uma by Como $$$ *Paro.* With excellent food and five-star service, this beautiful hotel restaurant has a traditional atmosphere and panoramic windows overlooking the valley and forested slopes. International and Asian food includes vegetarian and healthy options. Decent wine is available. Start with flatbread to dip in tamarind sauce or honey roasted pear with blue cheese, and so it goes, a feast for the eyes and taste buds. Expensive, but worth it for a special treat or a romantic dinner.

Dagmar $$ *near the children's park, Paro.* Tucked in a back lane, this conventional restaurant features an Asian and international buffet. Food is satisfying and if given plenty of notice, the restaurant might also prepare a hot Bhutanese-style picnic.

My Kind of Place $$ *main street, Paro.* This new kid on the block combines scrumptious food and a relaxing atmosphere. Try momos, warm bread and noodle soup, maybe followed by rice and mango dessert as you sit at conventional tables or on comfy couches. Plenty of light in the dining room, pleasant décor and good views. Friendly and cosmopolitan.

Sonam Trophel $$ *Tshongdue, Paro.* A traditional venue serving homely food, cooked to order so be prepared to wait. This is one of the oldest restaurants in town, boasting an untarnished reputation for its excellent cuisine, hygiene and friendly atmosphere. Try Aunty's *ema datshi*, her signature salads, noodles and appetising momos. Portions are generous and Aunty, the owner cum cook, will love to guide you through the menu.

Tou Zaiga $ *Bondey near Paro.* If you are looking for something different, this is it, a training school for chefs featuring a daily Bhutanese menu with a modern twist. A quiet restaurant, with sweeping views and a charming ambience. Not the usual run of the mill sort of place, but offering tasty, inexpensive food and if it is not too busy, a chance to meet students and chefs. Worth the 4km (2.4 mile) drive out of town.

Yue-Ling $$ *main street, Paro.* Unpretentious, wholesome menu, offering buffet and vegetarian options. Bhutanese and Indian dishes available, with lots of flavour. Try the vegetable curry, curly fern or corn bread.

Punakha

Bukhari $$$ *Punakha.* Prompt service and extensive choice of international and Bhutanese dishes. Top for quality, living up to the Uma resorts' reputation.

Chimi Lhakhang Cafeteria $$ *near the Divine Madman's Temple, Punakha*. Good food and good views. A cosy inn serving decent Asian dishes while looking across the rice fields.

Dochu La Resort Restaurant $$ *Dochu La pass*. A welcome break on the road from Thimphu to Punakha. Food comprises Bhutanese staples: four vegetables, rice and maybe chicken and nan bread. Slightly overpriced, but there are cakes, snacks and sometimes finger chips. The large dining area may be noisy at times but in clear weather, the views are superb, stretching from the 108 chortens on the pass to the high Himalayan peaks.

Lobesa Village Restaurant $$ *Lobesa village*. This quaint restaurant sits in a picturesque location, looking across the paddies to the river and hills, 20–30 minutes from Punakha town. The menu features tasty Indian, Bhutanese and Chinese dishes. Service is attentive but to avoid the usual wait, ask your guide to order the meal before you get there.

Thimphu

Ambient Café $$ *Norzin Lam, Thimphu*. This is the local favourite for socialising while nibbling healthy European food or trying out the delicious vegetarian options. The menu includes cakes, toasted sandwiches, fresh salads you can trust, pizzas, hummus and pitta bread or for something a little more substantial, check out the tofu fried rice or the fragrant Nepali Thali when available. The menu changes frequently. Drinks include smoothies and milkshakes and probably the best coffee in town, since the owner roasts his own beans.

Babesa Village Restaurant $$ *Thimphu Expressway, Thimphu*. True to its name, this cosy restaurant is located in an old Bhutanese house, up two, possibly three, flights of stairs. Arrive early if you wish to sit on a chair at one of two tables, otherwise it will be cushions on the floor. After a welcome bowl of butter tea, a traditional banquet is served in wooden bowls and eaten with wooden spoons. Food is organic and tingling hot. The *ema datshi* is excellent.

The Bhutanese $$ *Hogdzin Lam, Thimphu*. This comfortable restaurant near the clock tower serves a selection of local food, not too spicy but always approach the chillies cautiously. The restaurant is open to tour groups.

Bhutan Orchid $$ *Chang Lam, Thimphu*. Interesting food, so don't let the stairs put you off, it will be worth it when you get there, even if you have to share the space with the occasional group. Good spread of Bhutanese dishes where the spiciness is slightly toned down for visitors. Sample regional specialities such as buckwheat momos with spinach from the Haa valley or the hearty buckwheat noodles from Bumthang. Tasty food and city views.

Edelweiss Restaurant $$ *Wogzin Lam, Thimphu*. This 4th floor restaurant close to the city centre attracts businessmen as well as tourists. The menu à la carte features international and Asian fare while the buffet lunch displays a range of authentic Bhutanese dishes. The local mushrooms and fresh crunchy vegetables are always appreciated. Good food reasonably priced.

Folk Heritage Museum Restaurant $$ *Kawajangsa, Thimphu*. Convenient for lunch after visiting the museum, the restaurant serves Bhutanese cuisine and vegetarian options. There is a set lunch and a pleasant outdoor seating area. The most popular dishes are red rice and *ema datshi*.

Seasons $$ *Doendrup Lam, Thimphu*. Quality Western food and a welcome change for expats and visitors nearing the end of a long trip. Succulent pizzas with fresh toppings, heaps of pasta, daily specials which might include steak, and fresh salads to add colour and variety. Sit in or out looking down on the lively Hong Kong market. There are books to read while you wait and it's family friendly.

Zombola $ *Hong Kong market, Thimphu*. A fun place to eat and as local as it gets, sharing tables and queuing at busy times. The menu is limited, particularly for vegetarians, but the food is authentic Asian. The Tibetan noodle soup and momos are among the best and cheapest in town.

Wangdue Phodrang

Kuenphen Restaurant $$ *Nobding*. Above the village of Nobding, beyond Wangdue Phrodang, this is a popular lunch stop before the turn-off for the Phobjikha valley. Expect the usual Bhutanese fare. Eat indoors or outside and enjoy the views when the sun is shining. Try yak butter tea when available, most welcome if you need to warm up, if an aquired taste.

CENTRAL BHUTAN

Chendebji

Chendebji Resort $$ *Chendebji*. A riverside resort on the road from Trongsa to Bumthang, near the Chendebji chorten. Continental and Asian food on offer, the most popular being momos and red rice. There is a gift shop and a traditional wood burning stove, a bonus in cold weather. The river stones piled on the top help to preserve the heat.

Jakar

Café Perk $$ *main street, Jakar*. Perfect when looking for a change from rice and chillies, this lively café serves tempting sandwiches, pasta, pizza and even fries. But top of the list are ice-cream, cakes, muffins and buckwheat pancakes, real coffee and milkshakes. Sit by the window and watch the world go by in the street below.

Gongkhar Guesthouse $$ *Jakar*. Delicious food, plenty of variety and a lovely garden full of flowers in season, located 1.5 km (0.9 mile) out of town.

Noryang Restaurant and Bar $$ *Wangdichoeling, Jakar*. A friendly family-run upstairs restaurant with a selection of Bhutanese dishes; warmly recommended are the mushroom dishes and momos. Picnics may be available if given sufficient notice.

Sonar Yangkhel $$ *main street, Jakar*. Healthy flavoursome food prepared and served by friendly hosts. Lentil soup, fluffy rice, freshly picked vegetables and the occasional surprise such as ginger carrot curry.

Swiss Guesthouse $$ *Kharsumphe, Jakar*. Something different in a bucolic setting with real Swiss cows, own brewery and cheese manufacture. Attentive staff and home-made quality food, from freshly-baked bread to traditional cheese fondue. A welcome change for weary visitors.

Trongsa

Oyster House $ *Trongsa*. Modest but welcoming, this central restaurant serves Bhutanese and Tibetan fare. The menu changes every week. Glorious views from the terrace. Guests can join the local youths in a game of snooker.

EASTERN BHUTAN

Mongar

Wangchuk Hotel $$ *Mongar*. On a hilltop overlooking the town, this new hotel boasts a restaurant and terrace with a view. Adventurous travellers can sample the local eateries in town and roadside stalls on the way to Trashigang.

Trashigang

Druk Deothjung Hotel $$ *town centre near prayer wheel, Trashigang*. Decent food – and a bakery attached, hard to resist – but anyone happy to go local will find plenty of cheap and cheerful eateries close by.

A–Z TRAVEL TIPS

A SUMMARY OF PRACTICAL INFORMATION

A

ACCOMMODATION

This will be reserved by your tour operator in hotels or homestays approved by the Tourism Council of Bhutan. All included accommodation is of a good standard in Western Bhutan and fast-improving in the rest of the country. New hotels are popping up at an impressive rate, though this is still limited in the East. You find rustic but cosy mountain lodges, pristine farmhouses and homestays, boutique hotels edging towards four-star levels and luxury resorts. Top of the list are the exclusive Aman Lodges, set in stunning surroundings. Expect traditional architecture and interior decorations, and underfloor heating or warm fires in winter. Private facilities are the norm while most hotels provide drinking water, TV and Wi-Fi in room or public areas, most reliable in popular tourist spots. All have restaurants with a buffet dinner and sometimes à la carte when not catering for a large group. Service can be slow at busy times but is always friendly. Be aware that stray dogs often bark through the night, even in town, so if you are a light sleeper, consider earplugs.

Standard rooms in three-star venues and homestays are covered in the tour price, including tax and service, but superior rooms incur a small supplement. Four star hotels may charge an extra $10–150 a night depending on room type but for five-star luxury, expect a supplement of $100–800 per room per night and up to $1,600 in the Aman Lodges.

Prices vary significantly between high and low season :

High season: March–May, Sept–Nov

Shoulder: Dec–Feb

Low season: June–Aug

If you hope to attend a festival, plan early as hotels can be booked up months in advance and be prepared to pay a supplement in some cases. During the low season however, hotels often have discounts and this may be a good chance to add real luxury to your Bhutanese experience.

But as always, remember that everything in Bhutan is flexible and although you requested a particular hotel, it may become unavailable at the last minute. This can be to accommodate a group, which turned out larger than expected, and single travellers and couples are most likely to be affected. So if you have booked three nights but have to pack your bags after the first, don't worry, your guide will find you somewhere to stay and it may even turn out better than your original choice.

AGENCIES AND TOUR OPERATORS

After its inception in 1974, tourism grew at snail's pace until the Bhutan Tourism Corporation was privatised in 1991, gradually paving the way for the over 100 licensed companies now operating in the country, alongside many overseas agencies. All apply the same principle of pre-booked fully inclusive tours, for group or private trips, which can be tailored to accommodate customers' requests. Options range from cultural and special interest to adventure and trekking for all abilities.

Bhutan-based agencies

Etho Metho Tours and Treks tel: 2-323 162, www.bhutanethometho.com
Bhutan Green Travel tel: 2-333 083, www.bhutangreentravel.com

UK operators

Blue Poppy Tours and Treks tel: 020-7609 2029, www.bluepoppybhutan.com
Mountain Kingdoms tel:01453-844 400, www.mountainkingdoms.com

Worldwide

Wind Horse Tours, Treks and Expeditions www.windhorsetours.com

AIRPORTS

Paro international airport PHB, run by the Bhutan Civil Aviation Authority, www.bcaa.gov.bt

Bhutan's only international airport is 6km (3.7 miles) from Paro town and 50km (31 miles) from the capital Thimphu. It is the hub for Druk Air and Bhutan Airlines and also serves as a domestic airport for Gelephu and Bumthang flights.

At an altitude of 2,235m (7,332ft), it is set in a deep valley close to the river and surrounded by mountains climbing to 5,500m (18,000ft). Planes can only land in daylight under visual meteorological conditions, which means the pilot must have full visibility rather than rely on instruments. Pilots have to undergo special training to land in Paro and only a handful are qualified. The combination of high altitude, short runway, strong winds and mountains make it one of the world's most challenging airports. But at least the sky is never crowded and Paro airport has maintained a clean safety record, with all flights being subject to change if conditions dictate. Most visitors are unaffected, especially in the high season when the weather is generally reliable, others might experience cancellations or delays but either way, the landing, when it comes, is breathtaking.

Entry formalities are straightforward since visas are pre-arranged by the tour operator. Note that in order to encourage a smoke-free environment, cigarettes for personal use must be declared on entry and are subject to 200 percent tax, with a maximum allowed of 800 per month. Guides wait for their visitors after clearance with private transfers to Paro or Thimphu hotels.

Bathpalathang airport BUT
Jakar, Bumthang, domestic flights to Paro and Gelephu.
Gelephu airport GLU
Gelephu, Southern Bhutan, domestic flights to Paro and Bumthang

B

BICYCLES

A number of companies specialise in cycling tours but hiring a bike for a day is possible, though this may prove difficult at busy times. The best option is to inform your tour operator in advance and if that fails, ask your guide if this can be organised as soon as you get to your destination. Cycle hire shops (www.bhutanbike.com) are found in tourist areas but if you are doing this under your own steam, check the equipment, brakes and all, before setting off. The daily rate is from $17 upwards, depending on model and outlet.

Roads are improving in general and the number of minor roads is increasing, but be aware that away from the valley floor, it is all about climbing up and down. Traffic is on the left and generally slow, drivers are courteous but expect to meet trucks on the highway.

BUDGETING FOR YOUR TRIP

As trips are prepaid and all inclusive, the main expense is likely to be souvenirs, ranging from collectors' stamps to textiles and other handicrafts. The price depends on quality: for instance, a ready-made *gho* in Thimphu can cost from $25 to $90 for a silk-like item while real silk will hit the roof. Most imported items should cost only a few dollars but be prepared to pay the price for handmade Bhutanese craft.

Allow for sweet treats in the bakery shops and soft and alcoholic drinks not included in the package. A beer costs from $2.30 to $3.85, an evening meal in a mid-range restaurant from $14 upwards. Then remember temple donations and tipping for the guide and driver at the end of the trip. This is appreciated but not compulsory. Think also about the activities you might decide to add when you get there, like cycling or rafting, or maybe a last minute hotel upgrade if you feel like it.

C

CAMPING

This is available on treks and will be fully organised by your operator.

CLIMATE

Spring is usually dry, summer wet, autumn sunny and bright and winter cold, but expect substantial variations depending on the altitude and influence of the monsoon.

Below are maximum temperatures for Thimphu.

	J	F	M	A	M	J	J	A	S	O	N	D
°C	12	14	16	20	22	24	26	25	23	22	18	14
°F	54	57	61	68	72	75	79	77	73	72	64	57

Bumthang is noticeably cooler than Thimphu while Punakha and Trashigang have warm winters and temperatures approaching 30°C (86°F) in late spring and summer. The high mountains are cold in winter and cool in summer. The semitropical belt in the south is hot year round with heavy rain and high humidity from June to September.

CLOTHING

Except in the subtropical south, temperatures drop in the evening so pack some warm clothing. The higher the altitude, the more layers you will need, plus woolly hat and gloves, a must if camping. During the day the sun can be bright anywhere but is particularly fierce in the mountains so suncream, sun glasses and hat are a must. Consider taking a trekking pole, it won't do any harm even if you are fit.

Sightseeing involves a fair amount of walking and sometimes a lot of steps so comfortable shoes are essential.

CRIME AND SAFETY

Bhutan is a safe destination where the vast majority of people are honest and respectful. Scams have no place in traditional Bhutanese culture and the worse you might encounter is petty theft. This is still a rarity and common sense precautions will suffice. Keep cash, bank cards and documents safe and have a photocopy of the first page of your passport and plane tickets just in case. Should an incident arise, report it immediately to your guide or hotel staff.

D

DISABLED TRAVELLERS

Tours are demanding due to hilly terrain, bumpy roads and scarcity of specifically designed facilities. Special needs regarding accommodation or visits should be discussed prior to booking. You will find the Bhutanese always ready to assist but consider a travelling companion to help you face any challenge which might arise.

DRIVING

Few companies, if any, would consider hiring a car to a foreign driver and this is not encouraged for safety reasons. The high altitude roads and mountains passes are fraught with hazards from hairpin bends to precipitous drops, road works, landslides and sudden snowfall. Service stations are far and few in between and in case of breakdown or accident, it could take emergency services several hours or even a day to reach the spot.

So it is far better to let the experienced Bhutanese drivers take the strain and sort out potential problems. After all, this is included in the price and your trip will be more enjoyable if you sit back and relax, marvelling at the scenery and quirky road signs along the way, 'this is highway not runway', 'darling I love you, but go gentle on my curves' and other similar gems.

E

ELECTRICITY

The electric current is 230 volts. Electric plugs are either two or three round pins (Indian type) and occasionally three flat pins. Hotels may have adaptors but to be on the safe side, bring your own multi-adaptor, available in most departure airports.

EMBASSIES AND CONSULATES

UK: British Honorary Consulate, 2nd floor above RICB Colony, Thimphu, tel: 17 61 85 53, www.ukinbhutan.bt

Canada: Canadian Cooperation Office, Thimphu, tel: 2 332 109/615, canada@druknet.bt

There are 14 foreign representations in Bhutan, all in Thimphu except the General Consulate of India (Phuentsholing).

Embassies: Bangladesh, India, Kuwait

Consulates: Belgium, India, Netherlands, Sweden, Thailand, UK.

Other representative offices: Austria, Canada, Denmark, Japan, Switzerland

EMERGENCY NUMBERS
Ambulance 112
Police 113
Fire brigade 110

G

GAY AND LESBIAN TRAVELLERS
Same sex relationships are illegal and not commonly accepted. The law is not strictly enforced but discretion is always best.

GETTING THERE AND AWAY
By air
Only the two Bhutanese airlines fly to Paro. Druk Air (www.drukair.com/bt), the national carrier, operates flights from Delhi and other airports in India, Kathmandu, Bangkok, Singapore and Dhaka. The privately-owned Bhutan Airlines (www.bhutanairlines.bt) operates flights from Bangkok via Kolkata or Gaya and from Delhi via Kathmandu. Schedules vary with the seasons.

Tour operators reserve flights as part of the package but if you have a preference for either airline or transit airport, this should be mentioned at the time of booking. It is always wise, as many operators do, to allow 48 hours before a connecting flight, most important on the return journey, taking into account possible delays due to weather conditions. Neither airline has firm arrangements to transfer luggage. In Delhi and Dhaka, luggage cannot be collected and checked in from the transit area so a visa is required to go through immigration. The somewhat risky alternative is to hand over all your documents to an 'official' who offers to do it for you. In Kathmandu you can get a visa in the arrival lounge, then clear immigration to collect your luggage and check it in.

The most spectacular route is Kathmandu-Paro. Check in as early as you can, ask for a seat on the left-hand side, preferably behind the wing, and enjoy the most amazing flight along the Himalaya bristling with glaciers and snow-covered peaks. The captain will point out the black pyramid of Everest along the way, too windy on the Nepali side for the snow to settle, but you should also see Nuptse, Lothse, Makalu, Kanchenjunga and as you approach Paro, in clear weather, Jomolhari, at 7,324m (24,000ft), Bhutan's second highest peak,

Overland

The main border crossing from India is Phuentsholing in the south-west, 176km (109 miles) from Thimphu and a 5–6 hour drive. Alternatively enter via Gelephu in south-central Bhutan, 237km (147 miles), 9 hours or so from Trongsa, or Samdrup Jongkhar in the south-east, 180km (112 miles), about 7 hours from Trashigang. Your guide will meet you at the border with onward transport.

H

HEALTH AND MEDICAL CARE

Before you go

Get travel insurance providing cover for delays and cancellations, loss of luggage, money or documents, medical care and other emergencies. Shop around but check that the insurance covers all your needs. Trekking at medium to high altitude and adventurous sports usually incur a supplement. Declare any medical history and read the small print, however long and tedious.

Book an appointment with your GP or travel clinic at least three months in advance and check recommended immunisations. The only compulsory vaccine to enter Bhutan is yellow fever if you recently visited an infected country. Take your immunisation certificate with you.

Ask your doctor to prescribe a general antibiotic and prepare a first aid box for whatever medication you might need, antiseptic, painkillers, anti-malarial tablets as advised and so on. Anything which might arouse suspicion of illegal drugs, such as syringes, should be accompanied by the relevant prescription. If you are prone to motion sickness on mountain roads, pressure point armbands work well for most travellers. Unlike medication, they'll let you appreciate the scenery rather than send you to sleep.

When you are there

Altitude sickness can be a problem over 3,000m (9,800ft), a more frequent occurence among trekkers than accidents. The initial symptom is a persistent headache, followed by breathlessness, dizziness, loss of appetite, nausea, sleeplessness, disorientation and irritation. To prevent it, take it easy in the first few days, drink plenty of water and rest frequently to allow the body to acclimatise. Should symptoms worsen, it is imperative to descend to lower altitude as complications can be serious and even fatal.

Travellers' diarrhoea should not be a problem if you drink bottled or boiled water and keep to restaurants recommended by your guide. Hygiene is better than in neighbouring countries and as long as you take care, you should be fine. But if you are unlucky, coca-cola is often recommended by medical staff, promptly sorting out problems in 90 percent of cases.

Other hazards include animal bites but dogs tend to sleep during the day while snakes, such as the venomous pit viper or the cobra found in the south, prefer to keep out of sight. In rural areas below 1,700m (5,577ft), most of all along the southern border, mosquitoes can be a nuisance and a potential hazard, carrying the dengue and malaria viruses. There is no vaccine or medication for the former and even though anti-malarial tablets are not 100 percent foolproof, do take them if recommended by your doctor. In both cases, prevention is best so to avoid getting bitten, keep your body covered, primarily from dusk onwards and preferably with light-coloured clothing, use the best repellent you can buy and sleep under a mosquito net in rural areas.

If you need medical attention while in Bhutan, ask your guide to take you to the nearest doctor or health clinic, or a shop selling the appropriate medication. There are hospitals in all district towns but the best facilities are in Thimphu at the Jigme Dorji Wangchuck National Referral Hospital. As a guest, you will be looked after like any Bhutanese and treatment is free. Serious cases may be transferred to Bangkok where a decent insurance policy should foot the bill.

I

INTERNET

Most tourist hotels provide free Wifi, in-room but in some cases only in public areas. There are internet cafés in the towns; connections are good in tourist spots, but less reliable and sometimes unavailable in remote valleys.

L

LANGUAGE

The official language is Dzongkha, the language of the dzongs, spoken by the Ngalops in Western Bhutan. It is usually written in Roman script, though the ancient Tibetan script is used in religious texts. Classical Tibetan is part of the curriculum in the monasteries but English is taught in schools at all levels. Most road signs, menus and notices are written in both Dzongkha and English. Due to the lay of the land, divided by high mountains and passes, over 20 ethnic groups have retained their own languages. Most prominent among them are Tshanglakha, the language of the East, and Lhotshamkha, spoken by Bhutanese of Nepali origin in the south.

Most Bhutanese have some knowledge of English and those working in the tourist industry are fluent. You won't have to learn Dzongkha to get by but a few words of the language are always appreciated.

Here are some basics to help you along:

Hello kuzuzangpo la
Goodbye läzimbhe jön (if you are leaving), läzimbhe zhû (if you are staying)

Good luck tashi delek
Thank you kadinchey
Yes yö/ing
No (thank you) mî (ju)
What is your name? chö meng gaci mo?
My name is... ngê meng...ing
How are you? chö gadebe yö?
I'm fine nga läzimbhe ra yö
Where are you from? chö gâti lä mo?
I am from... nga...lä ing
Can I take a picture? pâ tabney chokar la?
I don't feel well nga nau mä
Where is a... gâti mo
Bank ngükhang
Hospital menkhang
Market thromkhang
Monastery gompa
Police station thrimsung gakpi mâkhang
Post office dremkhang
Temple lhakhang
Left öm
Right yäp
Straight on thrangdi song

M

MAPS

There is a dearth of maps in Bhutan and if you are travelling via Kathmandu, this is your best chance to get a map. Look around the bookshops in the Thamel district and be sure to bargain. Alternatively there are online outlets or check out the official maps for east, centre and west, at www.tourism.gov.bt/map.

Large bookstores in Thimphu sell maps but these can run out at busy times. If you can't get a city map, do as the locals do and rely on landmarks rather than street names or numbers.

MEDIA

Press

There are six newspapers published in English: *Kuensel*, *Bhutan Today*, *The Bhutan Times*, *The Bhutanese*, *Bhutan Observer* and *Business Bhutan*.

Foreign newspapers are not available at the time of writing.

Radio and TV

Radio stations include the state-funded BBS (Bhutan Broadcasting Service) and several private stations.

Television appeared only in 1999 at the same time as the internet. BBS is the only Bhutanese TV station but cable TV offers a choice of Indian and other international channels.

MONEY

The Bhutanese currency is the Ngultrum (Nu) subdivided into 100 Chetrum (Ch).

Notes: Nu1, 5, 10, 20, 50, 100, 500, 1,000
Coins: Ch25, 50 + Nu1

At the time of writing, the exchange rate is US$1.00= Nu67.

The Ngultrum is pegged at par to the Indian rupee which is legal tender in Bhutan, though the reverse is not so.

US dollars and credit cards are accepted in some hotels and major handicraft stores but this is likely to incur a surcharge. The Bank of Bhutan and Druk PNB Bank ATMs accept foreign credit cards in Thimphu and Paro.

Local currency can be obtained at a bank or at the airport from the ATM or exchange counter, where unused notes can be changed on departure.

O

OPENING TIMES

Banks Mon–Fri 9am–1pm (some until 3 or 4pm), Sat 9–11am
Government offices Mon–Fri 9am–1pm, 2–5pm, winter 4pm
Shops 8am–8pm or 9pm

P

POST OFFICE

Thimphu GPO opening hours are from Mon–Fri 9am–4pm, Sat 9am–1pm.

The cost of a stamp for international mail starts at Nu30. Post boxes are red.

The philatelic bureau in Thimphu is located in the main post office on Chang Lam.

PUBLIC HOLIDAYS

Bhutan has a large number of public holidays which follow both the lunar and Gregorian calendars. Some are fixed to celebrate anniversaries, others vary. *Tsechus* and other festivals are not included in the list below. They are also public holidays in the area where they are held and occur at different times across the country.

5 February Birthday of The Gyalsey, first child of His Majesty the Fifth King
21-23 February Birthday of the Fifth King
2 May Birth Anniversary of the Third King
2 June Anniversary of the Fourth King's Coronation/Social Forestry Day
1 November Coronation of the Fifth King
11 November Birthday of the Fourth King and Constitution Day
17 December National Day
January Winter Solstice
January/February Traditional Day of Offering

January/February Losar (New Year)
April/May Shabdrung Kuchoe
May/June Lord Buddha Parinirvana (death and enlightenment)
June/July Birth of Guru Rinpoche
July First Sermon of Lord Buddha
September Blessed Rainy Day
September/October Dashain, Nepali Festival
November Descending Day of Lord Buddha

R

RELIGION

The majority of the population practise Buddhism, the mainstay of Bhutanese culture. Temples, monasteries and dzongs welcome visitors during opening hours.

Around 25 percent of the population are Hindus of Nepali origin living in the south, while Christians and others represent less than one percent. Adepts of the Bon religion are both animist and Buddhist. The Constitution guarantees religious freedom but does not authorise proselytism.

T

TELEPHONE

To call Bhutan from abroad dial 975 followed by all seven digits (the first one is the area code). Mobile numbers have eight digits.

Area codes in Bhutan:

3 Bumthang, 8 Paro, 2 Punakha/Thimphu, 4 Trashigang.

For international access out of Bhutan, dial 00 followed by the relevant country code.

There are no public phone booths but you can phone from your hotel.

Mobile connectivity is good in towns. If you wish to buy a Bhutan SIM card in Thimphu (Nu100), you may be asked to show your passport.

TIME ZONES

Bhutan time is GMT + 6 hours. It is 15 minutes ahead of Nepal and 30 minutes ahead of India.

Thimphu	New York	London	Jo'burg	Sydney	Auckland
noon	1am	6am	8am	5pm	7pm

Bear in mind that countries observe DST (daylight saving time) at different times.

TIPPING

This is not customary except for guides and drivers at the clients' discretion. You may be tempted to be over-generous but avoid upsetting the balance in the local economy. Keep to the operator's guidelines.

TOILETS

Tourist hotels, bars and restaurants have western-style facilities, the best option for visitors. A toilet tent is erected on trek.

TOURIST INFORMATION

There are visitors centres in Gangtey and Lamperi but otherwise guides are likely to be your best source of information. What they do not know, they will find out.

Bhutan has no official tourist office outside the country; refer to the websites below or tour operators.

TRANSPORT

Bhutan has no railway so the most common way of travelling around is by road or on foot. However, domestic flights are on their way. Gelephu airport in the south currently operates flights to Bumthang and Paro while Yongphula in the East has been closed for over three years, but may reopen at some point.

There are a few taxis in Thimphu, shared taxis in some cities for longer distances and public buses making their way to Eastern Bhutan but you should not need them.

Private transport, short and long distance, is included in your package. Vehicles range from adequate to excellent and all drivers are experienced. Depending on the size of the group, the operator will provide a coach, a minibus or a car.

V

VISA

Visas are sorted out by the agent or operator. At the time of writing, the charge is $50. This is not included in the cost of the trip.

W

WEBSITES

www.tourism.gov.bt
www.kingdomofbhutan.com
www.bhutan.travel

There are few websites dedicated to Bhutan but agencies and tour operators provide comprehensive information on their own sites.

RECOMMENDED HOTELS

The following recommendations cover the main areas listed in this guide and include luxury options for which a supplement is added to the daily tariff. This is at the discretion of the operator or establishment and must be requested at the time of booking, likewise if you wish to upgrade to a superior room in a standard hotel.

Below is an indication of the supplement added to the tour price for a double or twin room in luxury accommodation per night in high season. Hotels without symbols are standard and included in the daily tariff but a superior room would incur an extra charge from $10 upwards per night.

$$$	supplement from US$500 upwards
$$	supplement up to US$400
$	supplement up to US$150

WESTERN BHUTAN

Haa

Risum Resort *Wantsa, tel: 8-375 350,* www.hotel.bt. A charming place in a scenic location with sweeping views of the hills within walking distance of Haa town. Feels more like a homestay than a hotel. Spacious accommodation in the new cottages, tasty food, friendly hosts and hot stone bath on request. Ideal for birdwatching and country walks.

Paro

Kichu Resort *Lango, Paro, tel: 8-271 646,* www.kichuresorts.com. Surrounded by farmland, this resort boasts a cool riverside location, 5km (3 miles) from town. Rooms are in cottages, cosy and traditional, though the deluxe options are worth the extra charge. The restaurant serves Asian and continental cuisine, including vegetarian options. Try the signature massage in the spa. Ask for a river view at the time of booking and pack a torch to find the way back to your cottage after dark.

Janka Resort *Nemjo, Paro, tel: 8-272 352*, www.jankaresort.bt. A modest hotel set among the rice fields framed by wooded hills. With its ochre-coloured walls rising above the greenery, it almost feels like a village house and in season you can watch the farmers ploughing and planting rice. Deluxe rooms are in the main building, standard rooms around the courtyard. There is a flower garden at the back and vine-draped pergolas. Don't expect luxury but this a lovely country place a few minutes drive from town.

Olathang Hotel *Olathang, Paro, tel: 8-271 304*, www.hotel.bt. Barely 5km (3 miles) from the airport and a 15–20 minute downhill walk to town, this traditional hotel sits on a ridge among blue pines and greenery. Although it is a fairly large complex, it does not feel like it except in the dining room, where groups sit at long tables for buffet dinner and breakfast. Rooms in the main building are set around a pretty court-yard, but most atmospheric are the wooden cottages scattered in the grounds. Those on the edge have the best views over the valley. Archery demonstrations can be arranged for an extra charge and there is a spa and fitness room. The hotel was opened in 1974 for VIP guests attending the Fourth King's Coronation.

Pelri Cottages *Olathang, Paro, tel: 8-272 473*, www.hotel.bt. Up on a hill in restful surroundings, the cottages are scattered among peach and apple orchards. This is an older resort where Tibetan rugs and warm wood-panelling add a rustic touch to cosy comfortable rooms. The cottages have small balconies, some overlooking the valley, and the restaurant serves Bhutanese, Indian and Chinese cuisine. It may be low-key compared to the Olathang Hotel (below) but it's hard to beat if you want to unwind at the end of a busy day.

Tiger Nest Resort *Satsam Chorten, Paro, tel: 8-271 310*, www.tigernest. bt. A truly inspiring resort claiming one of the best views of Taktsang, the Tiger's Nest, rising above the valley floor. Set in tranquil surroundings 10 minutes from town, this attractive hotel has slate roofs, oak floors, wood carvings and granite, such as the fireplace built by a French artist to enhance the dining room. The Bhutanese and continental cuisine is based on organic produce. Rooms are spacious, the cottages showcase paintings by local artists and the alfresco bar invites guests to relax while gazing at the iconic monastery.

Zhiwa Ling $$ *Satsam Chorten, Paro, tel: 8-271 277,* www.zhiwaling.com. Some 8km (5 miles) from town, this luxurious heritage hotel brims with plush sofas, colourful rugs, antiques and artefacts. The architecture is dazzling throughout and rooms are spacious with unrivalled views. The hotel has its own Buddhist temple on the second floor built from old timber rescued from the Gangtey monastery in Phobjikha. The multi-cuisine Lingka restaurant is open all day while the Gaway promises re-fined dining in a traditional setting. There is a tea house and the Mad Monk Bar. Spa, fitness, yoga and meditation are available. It is only a 10 minute drive to the Tiger's Lair.

Phobjikha

Dewachen Hotel *Phobjikha, tel: 2-325 714,* www.dewachenhotel.com. A low-rise crescent-shaped resort displaying the best Bhutanese architecture, framed by sweeping views over the pine-covered slopes and the valley where black-necked cranes spend the winter. Rooms are spacious and on a cold night you will find a hot water bottle in your bed. The restaurant serves the usual Asian and continental food, the bar closes at 10pm but at breakfast time, you get hot toast prepared on the wood burning stove. The Dewachen has a gift shop and can organise cultural shows, horse-riding, trekking and hot stone baths.

Gangtey Gompa Lodge $$$ *Gangtey, tel: 2-340 943,* www.hotel.bt. A superb property where everything is top notch from the sunset patio, where neck warmers are provided, to the outstanding farmhouse suites with underfloor heating, hot water bottles and real fire. No TV in the rooms but there's a welcoming fire and a free-standing bathtub with unbeatable views. Activities include darts, archery, cultural visits, biking and trekking followed by complimentary shoe-cleaning. Food and service are the perfect complement to faultless accommodation.

Punakha

Damchen Resort *khuruthang, Punakha, tel: 2-584 367*, www.damchen resorts.com. The resort claims a prime location on the river bank where birds twitter on the lawns among rose bushes and poinsettia trees. Upstairs rooms and 'oval rooms' have the best views. All are comfortable and tastefully furnished; size depends on category. Attractive traditional style both in and out. The resort is close enough to the new town to escape for a pre- or after-dinner drink but far enough to enjoy the peace and the babbling sound of the river.

Meri Puensum Resort *Wolakha, Punakha, tel: 2-584 237*, www.meri puensum.bt/punakha. This charming family-run hotel is set on a hillside. There are rooms in the main building and cottages on different levels. All are functional but comfortable, with balconies overlooking the rice terraces and the river meandering below by the hills. Some 6km (3.7 miles) south of Punakha, it is a homely place where you can tuck into a tasty dinner and watch the stars with hardly any light pollution.

YT Hotel *Lobesa, Punakha, tel: 2-376 012*, www.hotel.bt. A comfortable, friendly hotel overlooking the valley. The owner makes all the difference, a retired forester full of enthusiasm, keen to show you his colourful flower garden, arboretum and enticing orchard. If you love tropical fruit, this is a must in season, especially for the mouth-watering avocados.

Thimphu

Bhutan Suites *Changangkha, tel: 2-333 377*, www.bhutansuites.com. A short drive from downtown, below the Changangkha temple, this award-winning boutique hotel claims a serene location with valley and mountain views, plus birdsong from morning to night. Suites combine modern and traditional styles in soft relaxing colours, with large bathrooms, separate sleeping and seating areas and kitchen facilities. There is a trendy bar and tea lounge while the restaurant serves a wide range of vegetarian dishes and freshly-brewed coffee.

Druk Hotel $ *Clock Tower Square, Thimphu tel: 2-322 966,* www.drukho-tels.com/hoteldruk. A long established hotel, centrally located, extensively renovated but retaining its old world charm with cosy rooms and traditional décor. The shabby-chic High Jinks bar is the talk of the town as is the Indian food and the special Friday night buffet accompanied by live music. The Lha Yul spa, or 7th Heaven, has a selection of holistic Indian rituals based on Ayurveda. Be aware that the square is lively until late evening.

Jumolhari *Chang Lam, Thimphu tel: 2-322 747* www.hoteljumolhari.com. This renovated hotel fits in well with the traditional surroundings but inside are comfortable western-style rooms, carpeted and decorated in warm soothing colours. The hotel has a spa and a good restaurant serving a variety of cuisines. The real bonus is its central location, suitable for anyone who likes to be at the heart of things.

Namgay Heritage Hotel *Jangchhub Lam, Thimphu, tel: 2-337 113,* www.nhh.bt. High on the list of the tourist class hotels, the Namgay is located in a quiet central location, up a short slope from the main street, close to the shops. The atrium is impressive, looking up to the spacious rooms where modern comforts are at ease in a traditional Bhutanese décor. The restaurant serves continental and Bhutanese cuisine while the quaint coffee shop is a must for freshly-baked pastries. There is a small craft shop and most appreciated after a long day, an indoor swimming pool.

Pedling Hotel *Phendey Lam, Thimphu, tel: 2-325 714,* www.hotelpedling.com. A popular tourist and business hotel in a central location. Well-appointed rooms display warm colours and natural wood. The multi-cuisine is based on organic products from the resort's own farm or sourced from local growers. The Aru spa menu features signature rituals, impressive for a mid-priced hotel. The hotel is owned by a revered lama from Gangtey and the proceeds go to Buddhist institutions.

Taj Tashii $$$ *Samten Lam, tel: 2-336 699,* www.tajhotels.com/en-in/taj-tashi. Designed like a dzong, this is the ultimate Bhutanese icon but the elegant interior and state-of-the-art amenities are all you would expect from the brand. Deluxe rooms include sundeck and day bed, with the best views from corner rooms and upper floor balconies. Relax in the spa – try aromatherapy by candlelight – or keep fit in the pool or gym. Service is impeccable, whether you unwind in the bar, tea lounge or the all-day restaurant. Treat yourself to a traditional dinner in the Chig Ja Gye and if you'd like to add an extra touch of authenticity, you can hire a Bhutanese dress. In this oasis nestling in the pine trees, you forget you are in town.

Terma Linca Resort and Spa $$ *Babesa, Thimphu tel: 2-351 490,* www. termalinca.com. This appealing upmarket resort sits on the bank of the river Wang Chu in a rural setting, a 10 minute drive from the city centre. It is owned by the Fourth King's eldest wife. Low-rise, sleek and stylish, it combines modern amenities and traditional architecture from stone walls to wood panels. Rooms and public areas have large windows looking out to river and lawns, a flower meadow, pond and mountains. The semicircular Aie restaurant serves international cuisine, while the colourful, traditional Apa is for Bhutanese specialities prepared on a wood burning stove. Guests are entertained with folk music and dancing. Yoga, meditation and hot stone baths are available. The hotel has its own archery field.

CENTRAL BHUTAN

Bumthang

Chumey Nature Resort *Geytsa, Chumey, tel: 3-641 286,* www.chumey natureresort.com. A quiet resort on a hillside overlooking the Chumey valley. There are eight standard rooms and six luxury suites where the extra space is enhanced by the traditional décor. The restaurant serves the usual fare as well as local specialities. The bar has a sunset veranda and there is a gift shop, a temple where guests can meditate and an amateur radio club. Activities include village walks and photographic, cultural and birdwatching tours.

Kaila Guesthouse *Jakar, tel: 3-631 219,* www.hotel.bt. A popular hotel, lively by day but quiet at night, situated above Jakar, a 10 minute walk from the dzong and a gentle stroll down the road to the shops. This pleasant low-rise hotel has functional but comfortable rooms around a traditional courtyard. Guests can dine on Asian, Swiss and continental cuisine or snack on buckwheat pancakes with home-produced honey. The local Red Panda beer is on tap.

Jakar Village Lodge *Jakar, tel: 3-631 242*, www.bhutanlodge.com. Below the dzong and a 20 minute walk from town, this charming lodge feels more like a homestay than a hotel. Run by the third generation of the same family, it is best suited to guests looking for genuine Bhutanese hospitality rather than state-of-the-art amenities. It's basic but relaxing, rooms are comfortable and roses bloom in the garden. Enjoy Bhutanese food with an ethnic touch and lovely views of the dzong and mountains.

Rinchenling Lodge *Tashigatshel, Jakar, tel: 3-631 147*, www.rinchenling. com. A family run guesthouse offering superb value for money. Surrounded by pine trees, a five minute walk from Jampey Lhakhang, this friendly lodge allows guests to check in or out any time. Rooms are spacious, with wood-panelled walls, wooden floors and rugs, and there are two apartments. The hot stone bathhouse has twin tubs, perfect for couples, and there are flowers, lawns and a herb garden. Meals are based on home-grown vegetables and fruit and there is freshly-baked bread and home-made jam. If you missed out on festivals, the Rinchenling can bring in traditional masked dancers and musicians.

Swiss Guesthouse *Kharsumphe, tel: 3-631 145*, www.swissguest house.bt. This is an enchanting away-from-it-all sort of place, surrounded by apple orchards. There are two monasteries within trekking distance and you might spot up to 20 species of birds around the lodge. Wood-panelled rooms are functional but most appreciated by the guests are the delicious Swiss specialities served in the restaurant, complementing the usual Bhutanese fare. This a homely lodge, named after Swiss nationals who came here to work on a dairy and forestry project in the 1970s. Upgraded many times, it was the first guesthouse in Bumthang.

Trongsa

Puenzhi Guesthouse *Jorpang, tel: 3-521 197*, www.hotel.bt. Above Trongsa, a 3.2km (2 miles) drive from town, run by the former district governor, this guesthouse claims gorgeous views of the Black Mountains and the watchtower and dzong below. Standard rooms are basic, deluxe have more space but all have the same views. The restaurant serves multi-cuisine and there is a mini-library, gift shop and yoga or meditation sessions to help you relax.

EASTERN BHUTAN

Lhuentse

Phayul Resort *Autsho, tel: 4-510 829*, www.hotel.bt. In a quiet riverside village, this modest traditional hotel is a convenient base for a day trip to Lhuentse – 35km (22 miles) away. Six standard rooms, heating and in-room tea/coffee by request. Bar and restaurant serving Bhutanese, Indian and continental cuisine, buffet or à la carte.

Mongar

Wangchuk Hotel *Mongar, tel: 4-641 522*, www.wangchukhotel.com/wangchuk-hotel-mongar. Among the few hotels in Mongar, this is often considered the best so you may have to share it with one of the groups that venture this far. Rooms are comfortable and well-appointed, deluxe options on the first floor have views of the town or wooded hills. You can book a massage, a real bonus after a long drive. The hotel is just above the town close to the dzong.

Trashigang

Druk Deothjung Resort *Phomshing, Trashigang, tel: 4-521 440*, www.hotel.bt. Roughly 2km (1.2 miles) from town and not to be confused with the namesake hotel in the centre, this is a new resort clinging to the hillside above the valley. The panoramic dining room almost makes you forget the buffet food, and rooms and suites all have mountain views. Relax in the evening and get up early to watch the birds.

Lingkhar Lodge *Trashigang, tel: 77 11 67 67,* www.hotel.bt. On a hillside 10km (6 miles) out of town, this lodge has comfortable accommodation in quaint cottages surrounded by orchards and paddies. The restaurant serves hearty food indoors or on the terrace where the scent of jasmine lingers in the air. It's ideal to watch birds and butterflies and relax in unspoilt surroundings.

Trashiyangtse

Choki Homestay *Chorten Kora, Trashiyangtse, tel: 17 60 36 02* www.hotel. bt. A lovely spacious stone house, bright and cheerful with polished floors, auspicious signs painted on the walls and a traditional shrine. Serves Bhutanese and Chinese cuisine. Spacious rooms and welcoming hosts.

INDEX

INSIGHT ⊙ GUIDES POCKET GUIDE

BHUTAN

First Edition 2017

Editor: Sarah Clark
Author: Solange Hando
Head of Production: Rebeka Davies
Picture Editor: Tom Smyth
Cartography: Carte
Photography Credits: Alamy 4MC, 5MC, 71, 84; AWL Images 1, 79; Getty Images 4TC, 4ML, 4TL, 5TC, 5M, 5M, 6R, 7R, 11, 12, 14, 17, 21, 23, 24, 26, 48, 64/65, 66, 72, 74, 75, 80, 81, 83, 86, 89, 90, 92, 95, 103, 104, 107, 108; iStock 5T, 5MC, 18, 30, 32, 33, 34/35, 36, 37, 39, 41, 44, 46, 54, 55, 59, 60, 69, 91; REX/Shutterstock 42; Shutterstock 6L, 7, 29, 50, 53, 57, 62, 63, 77, 96, 99, 100; SuperStock 51
Cover Picture: Shutterstock

Distribution
UK, Ireland and Europe: Apa Publications (UK) Ltd; sales@insightguides.com
United States and Canada: Ingram Publisher Services; ips@ingramcontent.com
Australia and New Zealand: Woodslane; info@woodslane.com.au
Southeast Asia: Apa Publications (SN) Pte; singaporeoffice@insightguides.com
Hong Kong, Taiwan and China: Apa Publications (HK) Ltd; hongkongoffice@insightguides.com
Worldwide: Apa Publications (UK) Ltd; sales@insightguides.com

Special Sales, Content Licensing and CoPublishing
Insight Guides can be purchased in bulk quantities at discounted prices. We can create special editions, personalised jackets and corporate imprints tailored to your needs. sales@insightguides.com; www.insightguides.biz

Contact us
Every effort has been made to provide accurate information in this publication, but changes are inevitable. The publisher cannot be responsible for any resulting loss, inconvenience or injury. We would appreciate it if readers would call our attention to any errors or outdated information. We also welcome your suggestions; please contact us at: hello@insightguides.com
www.insightguides.com